THE ACTOR
AND THE
SPACE

THE ACTOR AND THE SPACE

DECLAN DONNELLAN

Based on interviews with Lucie Dawkins

NICK HERN BOOKS
London
www.nickhernbooks.co.uk

A Nick Hern Book

The Actor and the Space
first published in Great Britain in 2024
as a paperback original by Nick Hern Books Limited,
The Glasshouse, 49a Goldhawk Road, London, W12 8QP

The Actor and the Space © copyright 2024
Declan Donnellan

Declan Donnellan has asserted his moral right
to be identified as the author of this work

Extract from 'The Love Song of J. Alfred Prufrock' from
Collected Poems 1909–1962 by T. S. Eliot, published by
Faber and Faber Ltd, reprinted with permission

British Library Cataloguing Data for this book
is available from the British Library

Designed and typeset by Nick Hern Books, London

Printed and bound in Great Britain by
CPI Books (UK) Ltd

ISBN   978 1 83904 300 0

CONTENTS

1	Not True But Useful	1
2	A Starting Point	5
3	Sandcastles	11
4	False Friends	25
5	Green Glasses	35
6	The Crowded Space	51
7	Quarantine	69
8	The Other Space	85
9	Thresholds	97
10	Trying Out the Keys	111
11	Flow	133
12	Character	141
13	Predicament	161
14	Dread	183
15	False Words	201
16	The Political Actor	217
17	The Keys	221
	Acknowledgements	225
	Index	227

NOT
TRUE
BUT USEFUL

Since *The Actor and the Target* was published more than twenty years ago, Nick Ormerod and I have continued to talk about theatre and acting, trying to see what makes performance better. And more importantly, what 'better' might mean. The Covid lockdowns forced us to stop working and gave us time to think about what we do, and this book is the result. It is largely based on interviews with Lucie Dawkins, without whose patience and eagle-eyed rigour it would never have happened.

All the ideas in this book were developed in conversation between myself and Nick. The words are from me, and the structure is mainly Lucie's. It is a development of themes in *The Actor and the Target*, not a denial of them. Of course, neither of them is 'right', but they are both attempts to describe the indescribable from slightly different positions. Neither of them is a 'how to' book, but both suggest a different position from which to think about acting and theatre. They are emphatically not yet more rules to encumber us. In other words, they are not something to be got 'right'.

Nick and I never sat down to cook up a theory or a method, or to create a theatre company to put it into practice. Quite the reverse. We both remain suspicious of any theory. Over the years we have often been pressed about our process, but we have always resisted the idea that we even had one. Our belief was that we needed to commit to the specific company of actors with the specific text. So for forty years we have avoided any pre-existing theory casting a shadow between us and the work we try to do.

However, we have somehow found ourselves continuing to return to the same theme: the importance of the space. That is fundamentally what this book is about.

So, what is this 'space'? Well, there is no simple answer, but a story might help. Two young fish were playing, swimming around amongst the pondweed. An older fish happened to lumber past and remarked, 'The water's nice today.' The old fish swam slowly on. A moment later one young fish stopped, turned to the other and asked, 'What's water?'

We often take the space we live in for granted. And yet, without it, like a fish out of water, we die.

The Actor and the Target followed Irina and Alex tackling *Romeo and Juliet*. And now, twenty years on, they find themselves rehearsing *Macbeth*. We are going to spend some time with them in rehearsal, but it is not essential to have read *Macbeth* because this book is not about the play. Nor is it about a particular interpretation of *Macbeth*. Some interpretation will inevitably creep in, but please try to ignore it. The book's aim is to offer a different position from which to view acting and theatre. Irina and Alex could be rehearsing anything, but *Macbeth* seemed to us to be a suitable vehicle to discuss some of the more universal nuts and bolts of performance.

One last caveat: as in *The Actor and the Target*, nothing here is true. We just hope you find it useful.

A STARTING POINT

2

Human beings are actors. It is hard-wired into our DNA. From toddlers playing make-believe to old-age pensioners sharing jokes in the pub, we need to perform. It's an essential part of being human.

Acting starts early. We use it to develop our relationship with our mothers. We watch her in wonder, mirror her smiling and repeat the sounds she makes. She intones soothing noises. We copy her. We learn things by performing for her, and she performs for us. Does that mean we are lying to each other? Of course not. Performance is woven into the fabric of our lives. It's as natural and important to us as breathing. Performance is not merely a habit humans keep repeating across millennia, languages and cultures. It is more fundamental than that. Performance is what it is to be human. It is the operating system for life.

So, if everyone is a natural actor, what is the problem? Why can't we all walk on stage and just act brilliantly? Well, things don't work out so smoothly when you stand in front of an audience with an already-written text. In real life, most people can make a good stab at improvising their allotted role of father, mother, nurse, lover, and so forth. But give them a script, and their performance rapidly dies. This is the basic problem we face in a rehearsal room. There is a series of black marks on white paper, a dead thing, and we need somehow to bring it to life.

'Is it alive?' is therefore a continuing question in rehearsal. Now, although we can't define exactly what this 'alive' is, it becomes immediately obvious to everyone in a rehearsal room when a moment bursts into life – and it's equally obvious when it's dead. So where can we try to find this life? Well, we can take a tip from the experts. When scientists search for life on other planets, they don't look for living organisms themselves. Instead, they search for the conditions that life needs: for example, in our universe, water, oxygen, carbon, and so on. They find life not by searching for life itself but instead by looking for a *space* that could support life.

All life depends on context, ultimately on the space around it. A child can pick a beautiful flower in the garden, take it into its bedroom and later be disappointed when it wilts and dies. When a bit older, the child will begin to understand that the flower depends on invisible things – its roots, sunlight, water and healthy earth – for life. The child is attracted by the brightness of the flower but doesn't yet understand that, to live and grow, the flower needs a whole host of conditions which are not immediately obvious.

Everything that lives, including you and me, needs its context to bring it into life and to keep it alive. Imagine a megalomaniac inventor who wants to destroy the entire universe and leave only himself behind. He builds a mighty end-of-the-world machine. Then, when he is ready for his solo adventure, he presses the button. Hey presto! At that very moment he would indeed find that everything had disappeared. But also, at precisely the same moment, he would vanish too. He needs the world. Nothing survives in a void.

The space is the source of that precious life we are looking for in rehearsals, but we often forget it. This is not because the space is some difficult-to-grasp transcendental mystery, but because it is so utterly obvious. Edgar Allan Poe wrote a story called *The Purloined Letter*. Trying to recover a scandalous letter, the police tear apart a house. Their frantic and exhaustive search involves drilling holes in the wall and pulling the legs off a table to search for secret compartments.

But all the time, they fail to notice the obvious. The letter is in the one place they don't think to look: it is pinned right in the centre of the wall, in plain sight. And they can't see it for looking. Often the thing we desperately need and seek is hidden right in front of our nose.

So, what is this thing that we cannot see because it is so obvious? What is this crucial step we are missing? Like the fish in real life, you and I don't need to think about this thing, we can take it for granted, but it's quite different when we are acting another human being. Then we cannot take the space for granted.

When a scene feels dead, our first impulse can be to throw lots of energy at it. This is normally a disaster. When the TV isn't working, we can play with the buttons and dials all we like. We can even kick it hard, but ultimately it will never flicker into life. First, we must realise that the TV is unplugged from the electric socket. If the actor is unplugged from the space, the work cannot be alive. When actors struggle in rehearsal, they need to plug themselves into their character's space. And they need to do that *first*.

Actors sometimes plunge past this first crucial step and instead valiantly throw themselves into 'acting', meaning each word sincerely, desperately, deeply, indicating the slightest nuance and pouring energy into the performance. They can exhaust themselves (and indeed the audience), and yet it still feels dead. The issue is rarely that they have failed to discover the right feelings, or details, or characteristics of the part. The problem is simpler: the actor hasn't done the imaginative work to create a new and different space for the character. Yes, although the actor has no option but to be somewhere (there, in the middle of the stage, sweating), the poor character is nowhere. No effort can be alive if it happens in a vacuum. It's not just that the character is dead; the character hasn't even started to exist.

And this is what all the advice in this book comes down to. It's all about plugging into the space.

SANDCASTLES

3

It seems to us that our most important job as theatre-makers is to encourage the flow of life on stage. So it follows that we need to think a little about what the experience of being alive is like.

Is it possible to make a useful generalisation? Well, this one has proved reliable over the years: life is largely about trying to *fix* the space. From the very moment we are born, we are already trying to make things better. We can't breathe, so we take a gulp of oxygen. We feel hungry, so we scream to get fed. When we are wet, we cry. When we are cold, we snuggle up to our mother's breast. When we are uncomfortable, we wriggle. We will do this even before we can focus our tiny eyes enough to see the world around us.

To begin with, we don't have words for all these different feelings. But as we grow, our parents help us to label them as distinct experiences, called 'hunger', 'discomfort', 'fear', 'rage', and so on. We dislike these bad feelings, but they are tremendously useful. If hunger didn't feel horrible, we would starve to death. These bad feelings keep us alive. They also give us something to do. And *doing* is the very stuff of life. If the baby ever stops wriggling or struggling to fix a bad feeling, and is awake but completely still, it's a warning signal to their parents that something is wrong.

We have structured this book around a series of keys. These have helped us solve problems in rehearsal. The important thing about keys is that they are not sacred principles. They are only tools. Whatever you do, please do not turn this into a rule book for making a play. These keys are not sticks to beat yourself with in rehearsal. But when we feel stuck or discouraged it can feel a bit like being locked in a room. Hopefully one of these keys will unlock the door and release you. So let's take this as our first key:

- **A character is always trying to fix the space.**

This fixing will go on for our whole life. We never stop trying to make the space feel more comfortable. When we see a bully in the playground, we hide. When we come in from the rain feeling miserable, we put the kettle on and make toast. When the floor gets dirty, we clean it. Even in our smallest actions, we are always trying to improve the here and now. Of course, some of our solutions are more sensible than others. And even ignoring one problem, let's say a leaking roof, probably means you are busily fixing something else as a distraction.

But we are condemned to keep on trying to fix the space until the last question about when the next dose of morphine is due. All spaces are different, very different, but they all have one thing in common. No space is ever ideal. Every space needs to be mended, however slightly. Indeed, advertisers make fortunes selling us perfect spaces. Not because they exist, but because we would pay anything to have one. Sadly, humans can never swim in totally calm water; there will always be some turbulence.

- **The space is never neutral.**

Let's think about sandcastles for a moment. There are at least three things that are fascinating about sandcastles. First, small children don't need to be taught how to make them. Indeed, adults who try to teach them are normally sent packing. It seems to be one of those primordial games we are programmed to play. Secondly, 'sandcastle' is a misnomer, because it's not really about the 'castle' bit at all. The simple cylinder of sand shaped by the bucket gets scant attention.

The structures that really interest the child are the runnels and walls and moats that surround the castle. The child delights in watching the waters gurgle round, wondering at the almighty sea being harnessed and controlled within their structures. Thirdly, and most importantly, the child prefers to build the castle in the tidal area where the water is coming and going. They choose the spot where their sandcastle will be destroyed by the tide. They choose the annihilation of their own creation.

Strangely, of all the many things that disappointed me as a child, coming back the next morning to find my sandcastle washed away was not one of them. Like most children, I cheerfully set about building a new one. Yes, there are a few ultra-sensible children who build their sandcastles to last for ever, way up on the dry sand well above the advancing line of the tide. Few beachcombers bother to inspect them except for dogs with loose bladders. Children tend to ignore those sophisticated structures, with their posh flags and dry battlements, erected away from the destructive power of the ocean. They're built on water-free territory. Frankly, these castles feel safe, boring and dead. Most children prefer to watch the castles that are right on the edge of the tide. These are temporary, under threat, and therefore alive.

This is a game all about fixing the space. The children build their sandcastles in the in-between space between safe and dangerous, at the very edges of their power. They are bartering with the immensity of the ocean. This in-between space is thrilling because it is constantly changing. The tide keeps creeping up and down the shore, and so the rules are in flux. The children are caught up in a shifting contest of control over two things: time and space. They are exerting a tiny corner of control over the immense ocean, in a tiny corner of time when the tide is in just the right place for just the right fraction of the day. Just enough time to make a sandcastle, before it yields and is dashed to pieces by the waves.

This is the pattern of our lives. The space presents us with a series of challenges, sometimes small, sometimes overwhelming, and we are constantly trying to manage them. We must make peace with the fact that the world is always going to be more vast, more chaotic, more arbitrary and more powerful than we want it to be. We're just struggling to control the little corner of space and time that we happen to be standing in. We're trying to make ourselves feel safe. Just a bit safe, for now, at least.

Of course, another big part of the challenge is that the space around us is always changing. Nothing ever stands still. In fact, nothing can stand still. Everything is moving. Even a rock is just a very monotonous vibration. Everything, without exception, is in a process of change. And because the space is always changing, our attempts to fix it never finally work. We can never truly be in control. Our sandcastles will always be washed away.

Children who build sandcastles can therefore teach us a lot about acting and art and life. It's all to do with facing destruction and accepting loss, and understanding that the only place where life may exist is in the narrow borderland between order and chaos. Children find life by building their sandcastles in the dangerous space and not the safe one. All characters in all scenes are making sandcastles on the edge of the shore. They are playing with a tiny patch of control, in a massive, continuously changing world. All the energy and life in any scene comes from this ever-failing struggle for control over the almighty space.

- **The space is always changing, so the character is never in control.**

Let's look at the rehearsal of *Macbeth* with Irina and Alex. As with every character, the Macbeths spend the whole play trying to fix the space. And, just like children building sandcastles, they soon discover that after every attempt, a new wave comes along and destroys their efforts. The space refuses to remain fixed. Their sandcastle is never secure. They start the play trying to control the space. They seem somehow dissatisfied because they are not king and queen. So they fix the space by murdering Duncan and putting themselves in his place. As soon as they do that, they discover that the space doesn't feel more comfortable after all. So, they fix it again, and again, and again. They won't stop until it finally kills them (and a lot of other Scots). This endless sandcastle-building is happening in every second of every scene.

Let's look at the famous 'dagger' speech with our actor Alex. This is a moment just before he murders Duncan, as Macbeth lurks waiting for his wife's signal. It will help Alex to think that all scenes essentially have the same pattern: they are a chain reaction of the characters trying to fix the space around them. The space changes faster than Macbeth can keep up with. It's always hurling new problems at him which he must fix. He tries to come up with solutions, but ultimately they always fail. He never achieves full control. This is his text:

> *'Is this a dagger which I see before me,*
> *The handle toward my hand? Come, let me clutch thee.*
> *I have thee not, and yet I see thee still.*
> *Art thou not, fatal vision, sensible*

*To feeling as to sight? Or art thou but
A dagger of the mind, a false creation,
Proceeding from the heat-oppressed brain?
I see thee yet, in form as palpable
As this which now I draw.
Thou marshall'st me the way that I was going,
And such an instrument I was to use.
Mine eyes are made the fools o' the other senses,
Or else worth all the rest; I see thee still,
And on thy blade and dudgeon gouts of blood,
Which was not so before. There's no such thing.
It is the bloody business which informs
Thus to mine eyes. Now o'er the one half-world
Nature seems dead, and wicked dreams abuse
The curtained sleep; witchcraft celebrates
Pale Hecate's offerings, and withered Murder,
Alarumed by his sentinel, the wolf,
Whose howl's his watch, thus with his stealthy pace,
With Tarquin's ravishing strides, towards his design
Moves like a ghost. Thou sure and firm-set earth,
Hear not my steps, which way they walk, for fear
Thy very stones prate of my whereabout,
And take the present horror from the time
Which now suits with it. Whiles I threat, he lives:
Words to the heat of deeds too cold breath gives.*

                                              A bell rings

*I go, and it is done; the bell invites me.
Hear it not, Duncan; for it is a knell
That summons thee to heaven, or to hell.'*

Macbeth is in the dark, with the whole Scottish government asleep in the castle around him. And he's waiting. Alone. But suddenly he… sees something. Something that astounds him. He sees a dagger floating in mid-air. One moment, he is standing in an empty corridor. The next, he isn't alone any more. At the very moment that he needs everything to go according to plan, he discovers that the space is doing something wildly outside his control. This is a problem he must absolutely fix. He turns to us in the audience and urgently asks:

'Is this a dagger which I see before me,
The handle toward my hand?'

If we can see the dagger too, then he's not alone; there may be a logical solution, and he's not insane. Perhaps we can all find it together with him, and something that had appeared to be extraordinary could be explained away. But of course, we won't give him an answer as we sit politely in the auditorium. His attempted fix has failed. He scrabbles for a new solution. He tries to shore up his sandcastle. We hold our breath as we watch him search for what to do next. He decides that if he can grab the dagger, he can make sense of it, and maybe even sweep it away.

'Come, let me clutch thee.'

But... his hand goes straight through it. The dagger which had appeared to be all too solid turns out to be the exact opposite. The space has changed wildly, again, because Macbeth has just discovered that the laws of physics no longer apply here. What can he possibly do now? His idea for a solution is to try to have a calm, sensible discussion with the dagger. He points out to it that it is behaving illogically. He tries to talk the situation back under control.

'Art thou not, fatal vision, sensible
To feeling as to sight?'

No response from the dagger. That didn't work, so Macbeth needs a new fix. He tries to explain the hallucination away to himself and to the audience as a perfectly reasonable symptom of stress.

> *'Or art thou but*
> *A dagger of the mind, a false creation,*
> *Proceeding from the heat-oppressed brain?'*

Again, the dagger doesn't respond to Macbeth's logic. It's still there. New solution: Macbeth tries to measure it against the real dagger on his belt, to create some kind of anchor for reality.

> *'I see thee yet, in form as palpable*
> *As this which now I draw.'*

A pattern has emerged. Macbeth keeps trying to apply logic to extricate himself from an irrational and deteriorating situation, but the dagger continually fails to do what he wants it to. He struggles to wrestle the space back under his control. But it refuses to obey his commands. Indeed, the dagger seems to become increasingly obtuse, increasingly defiant.

Then, with a horrifying lurch, the space changes dramatically again. The dagger suddenly moves towards Duncan's bedroom. Macbeth scrambles to react.

> *'Thou marshall'st me the way that I was going,*
> *And such an instrument I was to use.'*

Alex knows he must make a choice. The space has changed, and his character must respond to it. But the nature of the response is entirely up to Alex. In other words, he must make a change, but what that choice is, is his to decide. Alex decides that Macbeth sees the change as hopeful, that the dagger isn't a bad omen after all, and it's beckoning him, encouraging him to kill Duncan.

Unfortunately for Macbeth, the dagger refuses to submit to his little act of mastery. It keeps flashing its warning sign with another shocking transformation. Now it's covered in blood:

> *'I see thee still,*
> *And on thy blade and dudgeon gouts of blood,*
> *Which was not so before.'*

Macbeth changes tack, fumbling for a new tactic to stop the nightmare. He tries denying its existence.

> *'There's no such thing.*
> *It is the bloody business which informs*
> *Thus to mine eyes.'*

All at once, Macbeth changes his language radically, as if he has stepped into another play.

> *'Now o'er the one half-world*
> *Nature seems dead, and wicked dreams abuse*
> *The curtained sleep; witchcraft celebrates*
> *Pale Hecate's offerings…'*

He talks about ghosts and witches and nightmares, as if he is trying to scare a child. Alex should never explain these words away as 'Shakespearean poetry'. These words are strange, but they are doing something. He is making himself believe he is the grown-up. 'I am not the one who is spooked, I am spooking you! I am the one in control. I am not the frightened child; I am the adult in control!' He is trying to out-spook the dagger.

The golden rule is that we should never ever leave our common sense with our coats at the door. Macbeth is a human being, not so different from me and you. Listen to the voice in your head that says, 'What on earth makes a human being talk like this?'

⚜ Pay attention to your common-sense alarm.

Shakespeare knew that we are often at our most human when we are acting strangely. In fact, it's often through our strangeness that we connect with each other. And Macbeth here is acting strangely. What is all this horror-film baloney? It may be because the space has become unbearable to Macbeth. So unbearable that he must exaggerate in order not to feel. It's as if he's whiffing some incantatory drug. He is using his words as a smokescreen to hide what he's really doing. And he's not just hiding these ugly facts from us, he's trying not to see them himself. It's very human. We often hide things by talking. We may notice this when we have an all-out argument in which we know we are in the wrong. We build ourselves a fortress of words.

Macbeth defends himself from reality by using exaggerated horror imagery. Suddenly, he imagines he is Murder personified in a medieval romance, and then again, he transforms into Tarquin, the tyrant of Ancient Rome, en route to rape Lucretia:

> '...and withered Murder,
> Alarumed by his sentinel, the wolf,
> Whose howl's his watch, thus with his stealthy pace,
> With Tarquin's ravishing strides, towards his design
> Moves like a ghost.'

Our common sense should tell us that he has moved into that most dangerous mode where we dissociate from ourselves. We imagine we are someone else. We are not the person responsible. Macbeth cannot bear to face what he is doing in the here and now, so he puts himself in an entirely different space. He wants to be anywhere but here, in any time but now. He transposes himself to someone who is 'there and then', to an alternate version of reality where perhaps he might bring himself to murder the man who loves him like a father. Effectively, he's claiming: 'It's not me murdering Duncan, it's Tarquin!'

Of course, it's all rubbish, so none of it works. Finally, he is driven to talking to the ground, the only thing left that still feels real and concrete.

'Thou sure and firm-set earth,
Hear not my steps, which way they walk, for fear
Thy very stones prate of my whereabout.'

The problem for Macbeth is that the earth is all too firm-set and real. The bell rings and that changes the space again. His wife has given the signal for him to murder Duncan, and he realises time is running faster than he can. He feels that there are no choices left for him to make. He must go and kill Duncan, now. For all his efforts to put himself in control, he's lost. The space wins. It always does.

FALSE FRIENDS

Let's look back at this soliloquy. Macbeth starts by hallucinating a dagger and ends up talking to the ground. That's a pretty good snapshot of a man in psychological distress. Alex may quite reasonably diagnose Macbeth with paranoia. And of course, if Macbeth himself went to a psychiatrist and complained, 'I have this terrible problem, I keep on seeing a dagger,' the analyst would probably deduce he was suffering from delusions and then try to work out what was causing them. Alex and the psychiatrist can agree that Macbeth is experiencing some severe mental health issues. Macbeth is hallucinating, and the dagger is a projection of his own guilty mind – somewhere Macbeth does not want to kill Duncan, and somewhere his subconscious is frantically throwing obstacles in the way of his path to destruction.

This is true, but it is also a perfect example of something that may be true but not useful to the actor. It takes psychiatrists years of training to understand how humans experience these things, and it's not for us as theatre-makers to dole out diagnoses. Our only job is to understand what this live experience feels like from Macbeth's point of view.

Macbeth's inner experience of the scene is that he is being extremely logical. Imagine a passenger on a plane having an anxiety attack that the plane will crash. Their friend travelling with them sees that it's irrational, but for the person in the grip of panic, it doesn't seem at all irrational. It seems logical that this hunk of metal *could* fall out of the sky. The wings *could* drop off. The pilot *could* have a heart attack. Inside irrational hysteria, you will always find a cathedral of logic.

Indeed, logic can be more sinister than we would like to think. Like fire, it is a good servant but a very bad master. Logic is a useful tool that becomes deadly if it runs wild.

Shakespeare often introduces us to tragic characters who are wrapped up in wild but apparently logical fantasies which drive them to brutal destruction. It's cold logic that makes Macbeth think that 'to survive, we've got to put Duncan out of the way'. It's cold logic that marches Othello into Desdemona's bedroom to strangle her, waving the handkerchief as proof of her infidelity. These men don't tumble into the wild madness of Dionysus. They tumble into the far scarier madness of Apollo. A super-flux of logic is just as dangerous as chaos.

All this proves a very good example of the fact that our job is normally the exact opposite of psychoanalysis. For Alex can't step into Macbeth's shoes if at the same time he sits on the outside diagnosing him. He should never, ever, let himself feel superior to Macbeth. We must always try to find complete horizontality with the character and the play.

Imagine a long tunnel running straight through a mountainside that is blocking out the sun. If you want to see the light gleaming at the other end, you will have to stand in exactly the right spot. If your feet are placed a little too high you will not see it, or if your feet are a little too low, you won't be able to see the light either. It doesn't matter how hard you squint and peer and concentrate into the tunnel if you haven't first paid proper attention to where your feet are placed.

This is the best way to approach our work. It's all too easy to be superior to a character by playing the psychiatrist. We can also find ourselves standing too low by feeling intimidated by the play, as, for example, when we tackle a great classic. One of the great challenges of rehearsal is to make sure that we are constantly shifting the position of our feet in order to get as horizontal a view as possible. Of course, this isn't easy.

It's a constant process of readjustment. It means we must shift all the time. It is all too comfortable to judge a character. Judging people is lazy and addictive. It's also very dangerous.

⁃ Get horizontal with the character.

There are all sorts of questions that creep into rehearsal rooms and stop us from getting horizontal with the play. The biggest culprits are 'Is this true?' and 'Is this realistic?' 'Realistic' is a very dodgy word because it has little to do with reality, little to do with how things really are. When we praise something for being realistic, it is always something fake, like a waxwork or plastic flowers. Imagine how rude it would be to say to someone, 'I really enjoyed meeting your husband. He was so realistic.' It's also an offensive thing to say about a living work of art. Realistic is merely what we imagine reality *ought* to look like.

Unfortunately, life doesn't often seem realistic, especially at its most dramatic. It never feels real when you drive past the scene of a road accident and glimpse a casualty lying dead on the tarmac. Nor does it ever feel real when you are pacing the corridor outside intensive care at three in the morning, with a loved one on life support. It would be very odd to say: 'This seems so real.' When we encounter something extreme, we find ourselves adrift from reality. And plays on the whole are all about extreme situations. They are often about how humans behave when we are pushed to our limits.

Realism is a con. It's a reassurance for ourselves that we are the arbiters of what reality ought to look like, and that we are somehow in control of it. Concepts like 'realistic' comfort us in the face of the absurd arbitrariness of things, and our tininess within the universe. All the word 'realistic' tells us is that we have a lot of presumptions and predictions about how we think the world ought to look, if only it behaved neatly. But the world doesn't behave neatly, especially in good plays. In fact, be wary of words with '–ic' at the end. 'Realistic' is what we think reality should look like. 'Artistic' is what we think art should look like. 'Poetic' is what we think poetry should sound like. None of them are to do with what art, poetry or reality actually are. Very often they are far apart.

The other false idol in rehearsal is the pursuit of truth. We can never pin down the slippery thing we refer to as the truth. Truth is distinct from fact. There was a case where an American woman had an argument with her roommate over a phone charger and stabbed her to death. Ninety-one times. In court, the question 'Did you stab your roommate?' has an answer in fact: yes or no. 'Why did you stab your roommate?' is a question about truth and can only ever have a partial answer. Clearly the response – which was, 'Because she wouldn't give me the phone charger' – barely scratches the surface of the truth. There is no possible way to explain fully what led to such shocking violence.

Of course, we must keep asking questions about the truth. It's very important that we do, but expecting to find a full answer is absurd. Perhaps truth exists. Maybe there is a great God in Heaven. Maybe She knows exactly what the truth is. But for us down on Earth, there is a plurality of so-called truths. There's my truth and your truth, how I perceive it and you perceive it. Truth is completely dependent on who is telling the story. When the definite article creeps in, 'The Truth' will invariably sabotage rehearsals. If you find yourself working with someone who claims to know 'The Truth' about the play, character – or anything really – you have a serious problem. For what ends up passing for 'The Truth' is just the story of the most powerful voice. It is the dominant interpretation. The word can't help but take on a whiff of sanctity and superiority.

We need to be suspicious of The Truth, but at the same time, of course, we need to avoid lying. However hard we try, we will still end up not quite telling the truth. But we need to accept this difficult aspect of life, forgive ourselves, and simply try to do better tomorrow. In court, when we swear to 'tell the truth, the whole truth and nothing but the truth', it's quite a tall order. It would be more humble and less vain to say we promise to tell the facts, all the facts and nothing but the facts, and that, as far as we can tell, we will not mislead. But that is quite a mouthful. In fact, many of our most dangerous lies are the lies we compulsively tell ourselves. And uncovering this very human mechanism of self-deception powers many great plays.

Any event can be interpreted in a multitude of ways. A good evening in the theatre should leave the audience in a place of ambivalence and ambiguity, with a more complex understanding of the world. A great production should make the most of the audience's capacity to reach many and various conclusions about what they are watching. We shouldn't patronise them by serving them one interpretation of truth on a plate. Irina and Alex can let themselves off the truth-seeker pledge. They can get off the realism train. All they need to look for is life.

So Alex can relieve himself of any effort to somehow perform a 'realistic' portrayal of Macbeth's paranoia. That will get him nowhere. Instead, he needs to get on with the humbler problem of trying to see what Macbeth sees. Although Alex knows that the dagger isn't real, this is not Macbeth's experience of the scene. To Macbeth, the dagger seems as real as anything else (in fact, it seems *more* real than anything else). All Alex can share with the audience is the carnal, concrete, immediate, in-front-of-our-eyes event of directly seeing a dagger. And only then, only after that, does Alex as Macbeth struggle to deal with it.

Alex must never, ever, try to tell us why Macbeth is seeing a dagger. (Nor for that matter should the director.) He will discover much more life as soon as he stops injecting the scene with his own energy and instead sees and opens himself to the changing space as Macbeth sees it.

⊶ There is no acting, only reacting to the space.

When Isaac Newton wrote his Third Law of Motion, it turned out to be great advice for actors: for every action there is an equal and opposite reaction. We never initiate actions. We only *re*act. Alex will have so much instantly available energy if he pays attention to the changing space, in all its intensity. Then all he has to do is react to it. He does not have to manufacture anything. He should have the sensation of standing on the deck of the sinking *Titanic*, bailing out water with a teaspoon. This is an unfortunate feeling for Macbeth, but a happy position for Alex. The more problems there are for the character, the better for the actor.

It's a key that should be a huge relief to Alex. He's a diligent actor, and naturally feels that it is his responsibility to power up the scene. But Alex must shed this anxiety. This anxiety is toxic for the actor. Never put energy into the scene. For if you do, the scene cannot put its energy into you. This is very important. Alex will only release a stream of life-giving energy once he realises that he can give up ever having to initiate anything. The space will do all the heavy lifting for him. He will find that all the energy he needs is already there and coming at him from the outside.

'Samovar' is a word meaning 'self-boiler' in Russian. Actors must not be samovars. Instead, they must get their energy from outside, from the space, from the ocean. The more dangerous and dynamic the space, the more alive the actor will become.

GREEN GLASSES

5

Irina is working on Lady Macbeth's first scene in the play. She walks on stage to read a letter from Macbeth, telling her about the witches' prophecy that he will become King of Scotland. A messenger arrives to tell her that her husband is about to return from the war. The king and the whole court are following hot on his heels. The entire Scottish government will stay the night. She's got very little time to put together the biggest house party of her life.

Enter LADY MACBETH, reading a letter

LADY MACBETH
'They met me in the day of success, and I have learned by the perfectest report, they have more in them than mortal knowledge. When I burned in desire to question them further, they made themselves air, into which they vanished. Whiles I stood rapt in the wonder of it, came missives from the King, who all-hailed me "Thane of Cawdor", by which title, before, these weird sisters saluted me, and referred me to the coming on of time, with "Hail, King that shalt be!" This have I thought good to deliver thee, my dearest partner of greatness, that thou mightst not lose the dues of rejoicing, by being ignorant of what greatness is promised thee. Lay it to thy heart, and farewell.'
Glamis thou art, and Cawdor, and shalt be
What thou art promised. Yet do I fear thy nature;
It is too full o' the milk of human kindness
To catch the nearest way. Thou wouldst be great,
Art not without ambition, but without
The illness should attend it. What thou wouldst highly,
That wouldst thou holily; wouldst not play false,
And yet wouldst wrongly win. Thou'd have, great Glamis,
That which cries, 'Thus thou must do, if thou have it;
And that which rather thou dost fear to do,
Than wishest should be undone.' Hie thee hither,

That I may pour my spirits in thine ear,
And chastise with the valour of my tongue
All that impedes thee from the golden round,
Which fate and metaphysical aid doth seem
To have thee crowned withal.

Enter a MESSENGER

What is your tidings?

MESSENGER
The King comes here tonight.

LADY MACBETH
Thou'rt mad to say it:
Is not thy master with him? Who, were't so,
Would have informed for preparation.

MESSENGER
So please you, it is true: our thane is coming.
One of my fellows had the speed of him,
Who, almost dead for breath, had scarcely more
Than would make up his message.

LADY MACBETH
Give him tending,
He brings great news.

Exit MESSENGER

The raven himself is hoarse
That croaks the fatal entrance of Duncan
Under my battlements. Come, you spirits
That tend on mortal thoughts, unsex me here,
And fill me from the crown to the toe, top-full
Of direst cruelty! Make thick my blood,
Stop up th'access and passage to remorse,
That no compunctious visitings of nature

> *Shake my fell purpose, nor keep peace between*
> *Th'effect and it! Come to my woman's breasts,*
> *And take my milk for gall, you murdering ministers,*
> *Wherever, in your sightless substances,*
> *You wait on nature's mischief! Come, thick night,*
> *And pall thee in the dunnest smoke of hell,*
> *That my keen knife see not the wound it makes,*
> *Nor heaven peep through the blanket of the dark,*
> *To cry, 'Hold, hold!'*

The so-called '*Unsex me here*' soliloquy is so famous it can intimidate the actor. But as we have seen with Alex, Irina can overcome that fear if she ditches the idea that she is responsible for energising all these words. Instead, Irina can rely on the space to give her all the food, all the energy, she needs. Irina's first job is to open her eyes to all the problems that are already waiting for Lady Macbeth in the space.

Before she even walks into the scene, the space is already throbbing with powerful pressures. The space makes nothing easy for the character. It is ceaselessly hurling something new at her which she must fix. Remember: we never act, we only react. What Lady Macbeth does in this scene is not some crafted plan of action coming from somewhere deep within her. Everything she does is firefighting, a constant attempt to problem-solve the space.

⌾ The space dictates how the character will behave.

There is an enormous caveat here. There is no such thing as 'The Space' with capital letters, because we each see a different space. The space is entirely subjective. Lady Macbeth will see a different space from Irina, even if their feet are standing on exactly the same spot. The world is unique for each of us, because we each invent our own space. We often criticise someone for being egocentric by saying, 'That person thinks they are at the centre of the universe.' But upon examination it's not much of an insult, because this is true for each of us. You *are* at the centre of your world, and I am at the centre of mine. Every character in every scene is at the centre of their own world.

The world is unique for each of us, because we each invent our own space. For example, Nick and I have lived in the same flat for several decades, but we don't see the space in the same way. Today, I've abandoned my usual spot on the sofa, and instead I've decided to write at the table. It is the same one I ate at as a little boy in my parents' house. When I look at this table, I see something that Nick does not. I am sitting on a chair that is a relic from Nick's family, so he sees it differently to me. This isn't just the case for objects that have a history. If someone is kind enough to bring us a bunch of flowers, we will each see a different bunch, because we are different people. Two people can look at the same thing but cannot ever *see* the same thing.

The space is so subjective that we can even see things that aren't there. On 22 July 2005, in Stockwell underground station, London police chased and shot dead Jean Charles de Menezes. They believed he was an armed terrorist. After the event, some of the frightened commuters reported they had seen a big object hidden on him and that there were wires coming out of his jacket. They believed they had seen a bomb. Afterwards, it became clear that the police had made a terrible mistake. Jean Charles was no terrorist. There were never any wires; there was never any bomb. This means that the witnesses saw things that they had not seen and remembered things that had never happened. They corroborated each other in a form of hysteria. It's shocking proof that from second to second we create the world that we see, and sometimes what we imagine is far from reality.

Irina needs to see reality as Lady Macbeth sees it. She must try to perceive what Lady Macbeth's version of the space is. Irina temporarily needs to stop seeing Irina's world. Whatever we think we see, one thing is for sure: it will never strike us as perfect, there will always be something to fix. Lady Macbeth's world will be full of problems that Lady Macbeth is desperate to solve.

Immanuel Kant suggested that we perceive reality as if we are wearing green glasses. If you have only worn green glasses your whole life and know nothing else, then you will be convinced that the world is green. Our understanding of reality is entirely personal, and it can be very difficult to untangle our perception from objective fact. Even the wisest, most attentive, most awake human being lives in a simulacrum, their very own approximation of reality. The best we can do is try to be attentive to our own green glasses, and never make assumptions that our point of view is objective. I am making reality up, as best I can, by imperfectly processing information from my senses. When Irina steps into Lady Macbeth's shoes, she is not moving from reality to unreality. Most importantly, she is not moving from truth to lies. There isn't a world of truth and a world of theatre. The world of theatre is made up, yes. But so is the world Irina sees on her way into rehearsal. We make up the world we see. Sometimes we do this reasonably accurately. Sometimes, as down in Stockwell station, and with tragic consequences, less so. When the actor acts, they are swapping one fiction for another.

Acting is not transforming into another person. This is, of course, impossible. Irina cannot actually become Lady Macbeth. But what the actor can do is to swap spaces with her character. Irina temporarily steps out of the space of her everyday life and steps into the space of Lady Macbeth. That is the nearest to transforming into the character that Irina will ever get.

⊶ Acting isn't about transforming yourself. It's about swapping spaces with your character.

So where can Irina start? A good jumping-off point is to start looking at some of the physical objects in the space around her, through Lady Macbeth's own brand of green glasses. Irina doesn't need to waste time dutifully ticking off every single object. It will not help her to write an essay on the light fixtures as perceived by Lady Macbeth. She only needs to pay attention to objects that will be useful to her and provide her with the most energy to make the scene explode into life. These will be the objects that are pregnant with problems.

A significant object is the letter. In Irina's universe, the letter is just a prop that the stage manager has handed to her in the wings. But in Lady Macbeth's universe, the letter is alive with challenges. The letter presents an opportunity: she and her husband are about to move up in the world. Surely, Irina might think, opportunity is a delightful thing. Sadly not. Imagine you receive an email inviting you to come to an interview for a dream job. You can't believe it. You are delighted. But it won't be just the energy of delight that fuels you. The terror that you'll fail and one of your imagined rivals will get it instead will be pulsating there too. The bigger the opportunity, the more terrifying the prospect that you will lose it.

This letter delivers an opportunity that will change Lady Macbeth's life for ever. She opens the letter offstage, and, as much as it thrills her, it also terrifies her. This is a problem Lady Macbeth needs to solve. Shakespeare has done Irina a massive favour. Before she even steps out of the wings, he has put her into the deliciously alive position of reacting rather than acting. The letter starts the scene like a pistol shot. It propels her on stage.

Common sense, however, tells us that this is an odd thing to do. Irina should notice that Lady Macbeth has come out to read a deeply personal letter to a bunch of strangers. But as we have discovered, strangeness is our friend in rehearsal. She clearly feels compelled to share this personal news with someone else. One of the many reasons we talk to each other is that we want to make sure we are not alone. When Lady Macbeth speaks, she is not just boasting about her husband's success. She's solving the problem of the letter. It has made her feel vulnerable, so she is enlisting us, the audience, as her new best friends. She hopes we will give her the encouragement and affirmation she craves.

So here is Problematic Object number two in the space: the audience. As soon as Lady Macbeth walks out to read her letter to us, she becomes aware of a sea of eyes containing a multitude of opinions which are completely out of her control. And she needs to get us all on side. Here's something new to fix. It helps Irina to use this key as a starting point:

☞ **Every soliloquy is a conversation with the audience.**

Since all acting is just reacting, it follows that we only ever speak in reply. Everything we say is part of a conversation. We never just speak for the sake of it. This is obvious when we are speaking to someone else. But we also have chats and arguments with ourselves. The point is, we can never have a solo conversation. A monologue is a misnomer. We always need someone to talk to because we need someone else to energise us – even if that someone happens to be ourself.

If you telephone the emergency services to say 'The house is on fire!', your words may appear to be about the burning house. But they aren't. The words are to get the fire brigade to do something about it. The words are not just a description of a dramatic event. You want something in return, in this case desperately. If the fire engine doesn't come, it will be a disaster. When we speak, it is a rule that we always want something in return, even if it's only a nod, or a flash of connection in the other person's eyes.

The audience are in the space with Irina, so why not use all that amazing free energy? Now, there are in fact two audiences. The one that Irina sees, and the one that Lady Macbeth sees. When Irina looks out at the audience, she will see Irina's own version of the space. She might spot a critic in row D, she knows her family is somewhere up in the gallery, and she may notice someone in the front row texting on their phone. But Irina must not see Irina's space. Irina must see Lady Macbeth's space. And what Lady Macbeth sees when she looks at the audience is quite different.

Irina needs to see them through Lady Macbeth's green glasses. Since it's life-giving to find the danger in the space, it's useful for her to see a possible hint of criticism in the audience's eyes. To have a conversation, she needs to see an audience that in some way may disagree with her. It is a deceptively simple but crucial fact that the audience is there in the space and Lady Macbeth can see them. It's up to Irina to rationalise this however she wants. Perhaps she thinks of them as the critics living inside Lady Macbeth's head, judging what she does. Perhaps she imagines them as the other half of Lady Macbeth's self, the part of herself she must argue with. Who these watchers are is up to Irina's imagination, but the one thing she should never do is erase these watchers from the space. Irina needs to put Lady Macbeth in conflict with the audience, otherwise she wouldn't be able to speak at all. She needs to dread the worst judgements in their eyes, but also the possibility of warm encouragement. Judgements she must fix, and encouragement she must fight for.

The odd thing is that the audience doesn't need to say anything for Lady Macbeth to have an extensive argument with them. Her main effort is to persuade the audience and herself that she is an indomitable, implacable force, unconstrained by what she characterises as 'womanly' tenderness. She comes out with wild, extravagant thoughts like:

> *'Come, you spirits*
> *That tend on mortal thoughts, unsex me here,*
> *And fill me from the crown to the toe, top-full*
> *Of direst cruelty!'*

Irina's common-sense alarm bell should be ringing wildly. We need to notice when someone, unprompted, starts insistently telling you about themselves at length. Imagine if a drunk stranger at a bar slid up to you and started telling you about how amazing they are. You immediately start wondering, 'Why are you telling me this now?' In this scene, Lady Macbeth tells the audience, at great length, that she is some sort of gothic diva, driven by pure will. She really, really wants us to know how ruthless she can be.

Presumably, then, when she sees the audience, she fears that they may think the exact opposite about her, so she tries to change their mind. Perhaps Lady Macbeth was always excluded by the cool girls at school. Perhaps she was the pimply one who had to eat her sandwiches on her own in the corner of the playground. Perhaps she was bullied. Perhaps she thinks that, underneath, she will always be that uncool, meek little loser. When she looks at the audience, she sees us seeing right through her, into the very heart of the things she most fears about herself.

- **All characters are unreliable narrators.**

Characters do not tell us who they are. They tell us who they *wish* they were. Indeed, they often try to persuade us that they are not the thing they fear they are. Even if they are trying to be as honest as possible about themselves, they can only ever give an imperfect picture of reality, because that is all they ever know. If I tried to tell you my life story, even the most honest version would only be my personal fiction. Listen to this apparently confident bravado:

> '*Come to my woman's breasts,*
> *And take my milk for gall, you murdering ministers,*
> *Wherever, in your sightless substances,*
> *You wait on nature's mischief!*'

Big talk. A real psychopath wouldn't feel the need to make this speech. She sounds more like a teenager who has seen too many horror movies and is regurgitating the scripts. The message of the speech appears to be 'I'm a winner', but the louder she shouts this, the more we can make out a tiny voice whimpering, 'I'm not a loser, please believe me!'

- **All characters are putting on a performance of themselves.**

Irina is a performer playing Lady Macbeth. That is obvious. Less obvious is that Lady Macbeth is also a performer playing Lady Macbeth. She's putting on a version of herself, a version of herself she wishes she could become. She needs us to believe her act, because then she might be able to convince herself of it too. All too often, to believe something ourselves, we need to convince someone else about it first. We often think (maybe unconsciously), 'If only I can get you to believe it, perhaps then I might be able to believe it too.' She needs to get the audience on side, to make herself feel better and to prove to herself she is not as scared as she actually is.

Lady Macbeth does not speak to express herself. None of us does. Ever. We don't speak into a void; we speak in reply to a problem. What may appear to be self-expression is always a kind of fixing of our space. Imagine somebody gets so angry that they must run outside and scream at the moon. This isn't self-expression, it's an attempt to make the space more bearable. Lady Macbeth only speaks to change the audience's mind.

Everything Lady Macbeth says in this scene appears to be about her and her husband. In fact, it is not. Everything she says is about the audience. For example, she performs a little pantomime for them when she creates an invisible version of Macbeth and gives him a dressing-down for being too soft to do what is needed.

> 'Glamis thou art, and Cawdor, and shalt be
> What thou art promised. Yet do I fear thy nature;
> It is too full o' the milk of human kindness
> To catch the nearest way.'

None of these words are about Macbeth. They are all about the audience. She wants the audience to see her as the powerhouse in the marriage, as a woman who can shape her husband to her will. When she says:

> 'The raven himself is hoarse
> That croaks the fatal entrance of Duncan
> Under my battlements'

we might be tempted to think that this is about the raven and about Duncan. Again, it's not. It's all about her trying to manipulate us to change what we are thinking. It's rather a lame joke. The raven's crowing was traditionally a bad omen, and she jokes that the one on her battlements has been screeching so loudly that it has lost its voice. She's trying to make herself appear super-in-control, the kind of cool customer who can make grim jokes whilst plotting a murder.

But there is a major difference between what the words appear to mean and what is happening. Lady Macbeth's words are about murder and spirits and ravens and battlements. But what is actually happening is her desperate struggle to change what the audience is thinking about her. The meaning of the words is merely the surface of the scene.

The most useful word to imagine saying before any soliloquy is 'No': 'No! Don't think that. Think this instead.' Here Lady Macbeth says, 'No! I'm not a loser. Me, I'm Mrs Big Time! Look, I can even control nature. The raven is on my side. Aren't you impressed?!' She's having an argument with the audience. Through her green glasses, she sees our eyes full of doubt. Every time she speaks, Lady Macbeth looks at the audience again, and realises that she has failed to shift that doubt. In fact, it's useful to assume that all characters only ever speak the next line because they discover that the previous one has failed. The words failed to put them in control of their space. Either their attempt fell short, or the space, as it inevitably does, has changed again and made the problem worse. We only go on speaking because what we just said didn't seem to work.

When Irina stops trying to 'be' Lady Macbeth and starts simply to see the space that Lady Macbeth sees, she will find it much easier to start work. The worst thing Irina can do is to imagine that Lady Macbeth can sail through lines like *'spirits that tend on mortal thoughts'* and *'unsex me here'* as if that's how Lady Macbeth always talks, as if that's how Lady Macbeth actually 'is'. Irina will torture herself by thinking she has got to become the kind of person who normally speaks like this. Disaster! It's much more useful to think that Lady Macbeth is speaking strangely because the space is forcing her to.

Everything Lady Macbeth is doing from the start of this scene onwards is a reaction to dangerous elements she sees in her version of the universe. Her drive is always to correct something and never to create something. She's reacting to the letter. She is reacting to the audience. She solves, solves, solves. She fixes, fixes, fixes.

THE CROWDED SPACE

6

You will have noticed in the last chapter that Lady Macbeth isn't just reacting to physical, tangible things in her space. She is also reacting to her own feelings, fighting against them all the way through the scene. This requires us to pause for a second and look at what we can find in the space.

It does not help to think that the space starts only where your body ends. Say someone becomes so depressed that they can't get out of bed. They may close their eyes and try to shut out the world around them, but they will only be able to escape by retreating into another space inside their heads. However futile or empty that world may seem, it is still a space. Our space is just as full of imagined things as it is of solid things.

✺ The space isn't just outside us. It's also inside our heads.

Even things that are inside you are part of your space. Take a headache, for example. The neurological fact is that it's coming from some chemical and electrical imbalances happening deep inside my head. Even so, that is not my experience. I experience my headache as different from me. I'll rub my forehead as if I can touch the headache, as if I can locate it as a concrete thing, a separate entity from myself. I have a relationship with my headache. I resent it. I try to get rid of it by taking painkillers or lying in the dark. I think of it as an enemy attacking me. It's a thing in my space I must fix.

Sometimes, when we love a performance we say, 'That actor has such inner life.' The phrase serves us well enough when we are chatting in the bar after a show. But it's deadly in rehearsals. 'Inner life' is a false friend to Irina and Alex. If you look carefully at any specific moment of so-called 'inner life', you will see that, at that precise moment, the actor is always plugged into something outside. Without exception. For example, Bette Davis's eyes were famously alive on camera. But it's not her eyes that were amazing (big though they were): it's what she saw; what she was able to see; above all, what she *let* herself see. That aliveness in her eyes was all about her reaction to her space. Inner life is a contradiction in terms because life is all about our connections to the outside. As a result, however much the audience may pepper their praise with the words 'inner life', it is a very dangerous concept for the actor to take too seriously, for it risks cutting them off from the life-giving energy of the space.

As we were beginning to see in the last chapter, Lady Macbeth's space includes a great deal more than concrete objects. She must grapple with the letter and the audience, but she must also struggle with her own thoughts and fears. The Macbeths both suffer from this problem. Their 'horrible imaginings' torment them all the way through the play, like rampaging demons.

It helps the actor to imagine that as many things as possible come from outside them and not from inside them. Our experience of life is that our thoughts, feelings or experiences come at us from outside. They are stimuli we react to. Let's take all those things we tend to think come from some mysterious inner place, and instead imagine shifting them outside into the space. Let's put them in the realm of 'things I can react to', rather than 'things I need to generate inside me'.

Emotions

Trying to act 'I feel [*insert adjective*]' is futile. Unfortunately, the English language is no help to us here. It makes us say things like 'I am hungry', as if the feeling is a part of us.

Other languages are different. The French say, '*J'ai faim,*' which literally means 'I have hunger', while the Irish may say, 'I have a fierce hunger on me.' These are much closer to our experience, which is that hunger comes over us like a wave. Even if you find it impossible to imagine that your emotions come from anywhere else but inside you, you will still be familiar with the experience that feelings rarely appear unless prompted by a stimulus from outside you. Something you see presses a button in you, and a feeling pops up. So instead of feeling some internal rage, it helps the actor more to think that something in the space enrages them. Feelings appear to come at us from the space, not from somewhere deep inside us. We don't generate them; we deal with them. Orsino in *Twelfth Night* puts it brilliantly, when he says:

> '*My desires, like fell and cruel hounds,*
> *E'er since pursue me.'*

He experiences his desire for Olivia as if it is a pack of dogs hunting him. His feelings are unpredictable animals beyond his control.

Feelings come from outside us.

Often, a feeling strikes us as a surprise. We are taken aback by its intensity and wonder where it came from. I may find myself getting unaccountably frustrated with my inability to break eggs neatly and lose my temper as I fish the bits of shell out of the pan. Shouting at eggs isn't a reasonable reaction to a minor breakfast-making hiccup. The feeling comes roaring in first, and I can't immediately put my finger on where it is coming from unless I make myself stop to think. Only then do I realise that it's not about the eggs at all. It rarely is.

At best, we glimpse the reasons for our feelings in retrospect. We certainly don't understand them. You can never understand your way into feeling something when you're acting, because you can rarely do it in real life. Emotions assault us, and we have to manage them in order to keep ourselves on track. We do not bid them, or will them, or generate them. We can only try to steer them.

You can try to work yourself up into an emotional state through sheer force of will, but it will always be false. The thing that makes you cry, or break down, or laugh always comes at you from the outside. You can't switch it on like a tap. If you try to generate feelings, you will never ever be able to do it, and will always fail. We all know how awful it is when people say, 'Why can't you relax?' or 'Why can't you cheer up?' It's paralysing. Now imagine the absurdity of asking an actor to summon an emotion like that in rehearsal.

We experience our emotions more as if they came from somewhere else, as if they are bullets strafing King Kong clinging to the top of the Empire State Building, waving them away as they pierce deep into his flesh. All he can do is try to hold on. Feelings don't come when you want them, and they always come when you don't want them. To steal a phrase from the witches in *Macbeth*, they '*will not be commanded*'. Anyone who is grieving will know that the tears won't necessarily come at the graveside. They are sure to come when you're least expecting them.

Many of us grapple with the anxiety that we aren't feeling the right things at the right time – or even worse, that we don't feel anything at all. There is a song in the musical *A Chorus Line* which ends, '*I dug right down to the bottom of my soul, and cried, 'cause I felt nothing.*' It's a line that often fits uncannily into the mouths of most of Shakespeare's great characters. Take Hamlet, for example. After his mother has married his father's murderer, he watches an actor from a touring company perform with emotional intensity. He turns to the audience in a torrent of self-hatred, tormented that the actor can put on such a convincing performance of deep emotion, while he, Hamlet, feels nothing. He can't even cry.

> *'O, what a rogue and peasant slave am I!*
> *Is it not monstrous that this player here,*
> *But in a fiction, in a dream of passion,*
> *Could force his soul so to his own conceit*
> *That from her working all his visage wanned,*
> *Tears in his eyes, distraction in his aspect,*
> *A broken voice, and his whole function suiting*
> *With forms to his conceit? And all for nothing!*
> *For Hecuba!*
> *What's Hecuba to him, or he to Hecuba,*
> *That he should weep for her? What would he do,*
> *Had he the motive and the cue for passion*
> *That I have? He would drown the stage with tears,*
> *And cleave the general ear with horrid speech,*
> *Make mad the guilty and appal the free,*
> *Confound the ignorant, and amaze indeed*
> *The very faculties of eyes and ears. Yet I,*
> *A dull and muddy-mettled rascal, peak*
> *Like John-a-dreams, unpregnant of my cause,*
> *And can say nothing.'*

Hamlet has the '*cue for passion*' but can't feel anything appropriate. It makes him despise himself. He goes to disastrous lengths to feel something, anything, but in trying to fill his own emptiness, he unleashes carnage in Denmark.

Many actors worry that they aren't feeling what they think their character should feel. Ironically, in many great plays, the character often shares precisely the same anxiety. They are just as terrified of not feeling enough of the right feelings. Everything the character does is an attempt to fix this. It should be a relief for the actor to remember that the character is as human as they are and shares similar problems. We all have a fraught relationship with our feelings.

◦→ We work against the space and against our emotions.

In short, it's not Irina's job to generate Lady Macbeth's emotions. In fact, her job is to fight them. Let's look at how this helps her with the '*Unsex me here*' speech from the previous chapter. She says:

> *'Stop up th'access and passage to remorse,*
> *That no compunctious visitings of nature*
> *Shake my fell purpose, nor keep peace between*
> *Th'effect and it!'*

In other words, Lady Macbeth herself isn't feeling what she wants to feel. Lady Macbeth's problem is not that she is some psychopath with no empathy. Her problem is exactly the opposite. Just like her husband, she may love Duncan, and powerful emotions of pity and decency are hollering at her not to kill him. In fact, Shakespeare goes out of his way to point out that Lady Macbeth does not experience her emotions as something internal, but as attackers from the outside space. She claims they are inconvenient '*visitings of nature*'. If she gives them '*access*', they will stop her from seizing the great future dangling in front of her. If she opens the door to her common feelings of decency and compassion, they will turn her into a loser.

And so Lady Macbeth tries to do what Irina, as the actor, must never do. She desperately tries to generate new feelings.

She wants to block one set of feelings and so summon others that will turn her instead into a ruthless killer. She wills herself to transform into a new character. She imagines forces outside her, whom she calls *'spirits that tend on mortal thoughts'*, and appeals to them to replace her fear and pity with ruthlessness.

> *'Come to my woman's breasts,*
> *And take my milk for gall, you murdering ministers,*
> *Wherever, in your sightless substances,*
> *You wait on nature's mischief! Come, thick night,*
> *And pall thee in the dunnest smoke of hell,*
> *That my keen knife see not the wound it makes.'*

She must keep demanding *'Come!'* to all these horrifying emotions only and precisely because they will not come. They won't come at all. It's as if she is complaining to the Amazon delivery man that he didn't deliver what she asked for. Unfortunately, we don't have feelings-to-order like that. Lady Macbeth will never win this struggle with her emotions.

Memories

Memories are also part of our space. Of course, neurologically speaking, we do carry our memories around somewhere inside our brains. Once again, this is true but not useful. This not how we experience our memories. We experience memories spatially. They hijack our senses and transport us to another space. One waft of the smell of burning turf and I am back sitting next to my grandmother in Ireland a whole world ago, waiting for the fry. Taste does the same. In Proust's *À la recherche du temps perdu*, a mouthful of a cake catapults the writer back to his childhood. Like all brilliant writers, he understands that the words alone can't possibly convey the full-body intensity of that experience.

In fact, memories only operate in the space. If there is a very dramatic event, we will often remember where we were when we heard the news before we remember how we felt about it. Those of us old enough to remember the attacks of 11 September 2001 will recall immediately exactly where we were when we heard the news. When a memory hits you, it feels as if that space is hauling you back. The space is in control. It doesn't feel as if you are riffling through the files in your brain, accessing memory from inside yourself. Instead, it's like experiencing a ghostly double vision. You may be here, but you are somehow, vividly, there at the same time. Like a clever ghost, a memory attaches itself to a space.

Memories are part of Lady Macbeth's space. Her space is populated with a memory of a dead baby, one with soft gums, which haunts her all the way through the play. Later in the play, we will come to discover that this is the baby she has lost. The baby keeps creeping into her speech. It can't be buried.

> '...the milk of human kindness...'

> '...Come to my woman's breasts,
> And take my milk for gall...'

The things we try to cover up bleed through. It's like painting over wallpaper, only to find that the ugly old pattern seeps through again. Those baby images keep surfacing throughout this scene as if oozing up from where she has tried to hide them. She wishes this was a scene all about being a hardened villainess about to step into her glorious future, a future of success, achievement and the sheer power of her will. But the space is full of the memory of that dead baby, inconveniently reminding her that she isn't that person without feelings. In fact, Lady Macbeth is top-full of ordinary human compassion. She's a young grieving mother, but like many of us, she can't bear to let herself be who she is. It is useless for Irina to imagine that Lady Macbeth's memories are passive images sitting patiently inside her mind waiting to be remembered. Quite the reverse: the ghost baby is stalking her, and Lady Macbeth must slam each door on this intruder and keep it out of her space at all costs.

Ideas

In the playing field of the space, we also have ideas. Ideas have an uncanny knack of turning into presences that start to feel all too real. There are many good words for this process: to *incorporate*, to *incarnate*, to *embody*. Imagine a husband and wife are having a conversation in their kitchen about how they feel. She admits to feeling trapped. He says he has been feeling the same. They both feel a bit sick. Gradually, they start to talk around the subject, and even about the possibility of separating. The wife reveals she has thought about contacting a solicitor, just in case. They vehemently agree that if they do separate, they must be civilised, proceed with humanity and respect for each other, and keep it all amicable to minimise the impact on little Martin and Mary. By the time they have finished the washing-up they are exhausted but have still reached no firm conclusion.

The process is gradual, but that night something strange happens. When they get into bed, they discover that they are not alone. There is a dark shadowy shape between them. The shape's name is 'The Divorce'. It has cold breath. From now on it will be loyal and will never leave their side. Neither of them knows exactly when the idea took on flesh, but a clear sign is when the form of their questions changed. Their conversation no longer starts with 'What do we want to do?'

or 'What do you feel?' The strange new question is: 'What are we going to do about The Divorce?' The dark shape has stopped being an idea, or a theory, or a vague sense of feeling trapped. It is now an actual 'it'. Every day it grows bigger and demands more and more attention and food.

A war is like that. It starts with diplomatic problems. Troops amass at borders, and perhaps both sides attack each other, normally out of some sense of self-defence. A line gets crossed, and problems at a border become 'The War'. The two sides discover that they have conceived a monstrous baby, and that baby has grown and grown and grown. Soon it takes over. It passes a point where the combatants can control it. It has momentum and power of its own. The question is no longer 'What do we want?' Now it has become 'What should we do about The War?' Perhaps this is a reason why it is very easy to start a war, and very difficult to end one.

We invent ideas to serve our needs, imagining we can control what we create, but, imperceptibly, the relationship between servant and master blurs and finally gets reversed. Like many beings that want to flourish, the idea develops and demands food, and if it doesn't get attention, it gets angry. Above all, it dreads its own annihilation and will not let itself be destroyed, even long after we have forgotten the reasons for its original conception. All our power gets lost to this thing we have created. Great and terrible ideas seem to take on their own independent existence. Self-obsessed, they haunt the space as if they have a physical body. We often discover that we can no longer control the baby we have conceived. We are no longer the master; we have become the servant.

This is painfully clear as soon as Lady Macbeth reads that letter. An idea takes on flesh. It is called 'Murdering Duncan', and it will suck up more and more oxygen between her and her husband. It will feel to them like a living thing that is lurking around the castle, an unpleasant house guest who refuses to leave. Soon after they have brought 'Murdering Duncan' into being in their imaginations, it's as if they can no longer control it. Eventually, it will become so powerful that they can't stop it. They pass a point and become too frightened to say, 'You know what? Let's not do it!' It's gone too far, and it seems to be impossible to turn back.

Let's look at what happens in our scene with Irina after Lady Macbeth has read the letter. Macbeth arrives home as the conquering hero.

LADY MACBETH
Great Glamis! Worthy Cawdor!
Greater than both, by the all-hail hereafter!
Thy letters have transported me beyond
This ignorant present, and I feel now
The future in the instant.

MACBETH
My dearest love,
Duncan comes here tonight.

LADY MACBETH
And when goes hence?

MACBETH
Tomorrow, as he purposes.

LADY MACBETH
O, never
Shall sun that morrow see!
Your face, my thane, is as a book where men
May read strange matters. To beguile the time,
Look like the time; bear welcome in your eye,

> *Your hand, your tongue; look like the innocent flower,*
> *But be the serpent under't. He that's coming*
> *Must be provided for; and you shall put*
> *This night's great business into my dispatch,*
> *Which shall to all our nights and days to come*
> *Give solely sovereign sway and masterdom.*

MACBETH
> *We will speak further.*

LADY MACBETH
> *Only look up clear;*
> *To alter favour ever is to fear.*
> *Leave all the rest to me.*

This should be a joyous reunion between a couple parted by war. Her husband's alive! He's a war hero! Do they run into each other's arms and kiss each other, passionately grateful? No, the scene doesn't go like that at all. There is now an ugly interloper loitering around the edges of the scene. It sounds rather more like a break-up than a couple lovingly reuniting. He hardly says anything, and she speaks in bizarre euphemisms. Neither of them knows how on earth to interact with the other because the strange new house guest, called 'Murdering Duncan', is breathing down their necks. It swallows so much space between them that they spend the whole scene tiptoeing around the idea. Perhaps each is clinging to the hope that the other will dare to put words to the terrible thing. But neither of them can. Shakespeare is particularly brilliant at indication by absence, subtracting something so we feel it more. The Macbeths talk around it so much because the idea called 'Murdering Duncan' has already become a third person in their marriage.

'I' and 'me'

At this point, Irina might reasonably ask, 'Well, if ideas, emotions and memories are all part of the space, then what's left of Lady Macbeth? Is everything just… the space?' No. Of course not. There is something left, but it's only a little thing – let's call it 'I'. It's nothing more than the tiny centre of consciousness, the little piece of you that experiences the space around it and decides how to respond. The space fires problems at this little 'I', and the 'I' reacts. It has an enormous sense of will, but it's minuscule compared to the space.

It's important to accept that 'I' can never generate any energy at all. 'I' can originate nothing. It can only react. 'I' is the tiny experiencer at the heart of ourselves. However tiny it is, it is the only part of us that can make a choice. But it is tiny.

Of all the problems that 'I' has to deal with, perhaps the biggest of them all is called 'me'. 'I' is never alone. 'I' always has 'me' for company, and it's often a fractious relationship. How often do you think, for example, 'I hate myself for having done that,' or ask yourself, 'Why am I being so embarrassing?' or tell yourself to calm down, slow down, or concentrate, as if you are talking to a child? When things go wrong, we often feel like we are handcuffed to an idiot version of ourselves.

◈— **All characters have a problem with themselves.**

It's useful to imagine that a character wishes that they had different feelings, could deal with things differently, or maybe even, at extreme moments, wishes that they were someone else entirely. Whatever they may say, all characters have some problem with 'me'.

There may well exist people in the world who are totally comfortable with themselves, but I haven't met one in any play worth putting on a stage. They don't make for interesting stories. Occasionally, a character appears to be entirely happy with themselves; but only to begin with, before they discover painfully that this isn't so. Benedick, in *Much Ado About Nothing*, starts the play swaggering around with his army officer chums, apparently very pleased with himself, laughing at idiots stupid enough for romance. We're not surprised when it takes almost nothing for him to fall '*horribly in love*' with Beatrice. The breathtaking speed of his total conversion shows that all that braggadocio was a thin veneer, a self-deceiving mask. Benedick is not a portrait of a man who is content with himself, however loudly he performs it at the start. Like all Shakespeare's protagonists, he is a disaster waiting to happen. Being a comedy, it's a disaster that delights us.

Lady Macbeth has a particularly problematic relationship with the person she calls 'me'. Yes, her great project in the play is her own husband. She tells us lot about this, but she has an even greater, and more hidden project, and that is herself. She's terrified that she may not be up to the task of getting Duncan killed. She feels some weak version of herself is holding her back. This loser is right there inside her; this loser is a danger to herself. Like Sally Bowles sings in *Cabaret*, '*Everybody loves a winner, so nobody loved me.*' The 'I' of Lady Macbeth wants 'me' to be someone else, the winner, someone hard enough to be '*top-full of direst cruelty*'. So she struggles to become someone she is not.

In her soliloquy, she maps out the qualities of this new superwoman she will become, ruled exclusively by her own will, who can be whoever she wants to be, like transformative exercises from some demonic self-help book. When Irina looks through Lady Macbeth's eyes, she needs to see the old 'me' that Lady Macbeth is grappling with. This 'me' is not some abstract concept of her deep internal self, her inner truth. This passive, ineffectual-nobody version of her feels very real for Lady Macbeth, someone in the space she must wrestle to the ground.

Irina has now discovered that she can find all sorts of things to react to in Lady Macbeth's space.

People
Objects
Thoughts
Feelings
Memories
Ideas
'Me'

The sum of all these shifting, changing, confusing, unsatisfactory, colliding things comprise Lady Macbeth's space. This is a nightmare of complexity for Lady Macbeth, but great news for Irina. The actor has no need to generate any emotions, no need to create some inner life, no need to power up the scene. She must just react to things in the space. All she needs to do is to look outside herself. That is where she'll always be able to find her next surprise, her next problem, already there and waiting to be fixed.

QUARANTINE

7

So far, Alex and Irina have searched in the space for life-giving stimuli. Good. But also, strangely, they can find masses of energy when they pay attention to what is *not* in the space.

Life is a continual process of inclusion and exclusion. Let's go back in time and try to imagine what it would be like swimming around in the primordial goo. Most globules never saw the light of day, but a very few lucky ones happened to create a sort of wall. This divided the inside from the outside – living matter inside and generalised goo kept outside. All life depends on this wall. The wall was a semipermeable membrane, which means it could let some stuff in and keep other stuff out. It let sustenance like food and oxygen in, and kept toxins out. It both included and it excluded. These lucky globules are our far-distant ancestors. A foundation of life is to do with deciding what to keep in and what to keep out.

In day-to-day life, we like to make ourselves feel safe by keeping out anything that might cause us pain or discomfort. There are things we want here in our space with us, and things we want kept well outside. It is the same in our homes, in our relationships, in our work, or in our heads. We want fresh water from the tap but not a deluge from a leak in the roof. We want to seal our homes from draughts but let in the breeze on a hot day. We want to lock out burglars but let in friends. We saw this basic pattern in the child building the sandcastle. The game is all about that moat allowing some of the water in, while keeping the rest of the ocean out. There is an eternal and inescapable pattern of inclusion and exclusion. We are constantly quarantining our space.

This also applies to our feelings. As we have discovered, feelings can seem just as real as physical, concrete things. So we want to keep pleasant feelings in and keep painful ones out. We sometimes experience our emotions as intrusive and inconvenient. Just having a conversation with someone else all too often involves blocking out certain feelings in order to communicate clearly. For example, we often must tell ourselves, 'I am not going to cry,' 'I am going to keep calm,' or sometimes, 'I am not going to laugh.' There are so many feelings that we want to lock out of the most mundane of interactions. This is not a question of being dishonest. It's a very human process of managing our interactions with the world.

As Irina discovered, Lady Macbeth isn't only reacting to things in her space: there are also other things that she is trying to keep out. Such feelings as her own anxieties, or that persistent memory of the dead baby. Like the rest of us, she tries to include some things and to exclude others. This business of inclusion and exclusion is a defining feature of all human interactions, of all life.

We have a need to exclude. Imagine two lovers in a field at night. It is dark and there is no one around for miles. Suddenly, one of them asks loudly, 'Why on earth are we whispering?' and the other bursts out laughing. Then they start talking loudly, joking at their irrational need for secrecy. Why whisper when they have nothing to hide and no one to hide from?! However, when the laughter dies away, and in order to get back to the business in hand, they will still have to lower their voices once again, not because they fear that someone else may overhear – they don't need to keep their relationship secret – but simply because they still need the fiction that someone *might* overhear. Most of us need that sense of exclusion to generate any intimacy in the first place. To include each other, we must exclude someone else, even if this 'someone else' is imagined. That most intimate act needs a sense of privacy and therefore exclusion.

A strange principle emerges: you can't include anything without excluding something or someone else. Inclusion and exclusion go hand in hand. This is a useful tool when it comes to exploring all relationships between characters. The script of a play is only ever one side of a coin. It tells you what the characters want to include in the portrait of themselves they are presenting to the world. But they can't include anything without excluding something else. And, even more importantly, the thing they are excluding is often the very thing powering the life of the scene. When a photographer composes a photograph, they are not only choosing what to put in the frame, but also what to leave out. A good photographer – like a poet, or any artist – knows what to exclude. The image is defined by where it is cropped. Every film is invisibly shaped by the footage left on the cutting-room floor.

 Listen carefully for anything that is loud by its absence.

The things that are absent are often great originators of energy. Locking them out often requires an act of violence. These absent things can control the action and consequently loom large over life on stage. So we need to be conscious of them. When we look at a scene, what's not there is often just as important as what is there. Nothing exists without its opposite. You can't have a play about honour that isn't also about shame, even if the word 'shame' is never uttered in the script.

Absence and violence are deeply interconnected. Exclusion is often a brutal act and tells us a lot about what is going on in a scene. Gertrude sees her son Hamlet grieving for his dead father, and asks him, very publicly:

'Why seems it so particular with thee?'

In other words, 'What makes *you* so special? What makes your grief any different from anyone else's?' It is the absence, what she is *not* saying to her child, that makes this line so cruel. She leaves out motherly love; she leaves out comfort and empathy.

At the end of Chekhov's play *Three Sisters*, the character of Tusenbach (the fiancé of the youngest sister Irina) gets killed in a duel. The sisters know it's going to happen and do nothing to stop it. The doctor, who might have been able to help, chatters away inconsequentially, '*One baron more, one baron less…*' Right in the middle of the scene, they hear the gunshot that kills Tusenbach. His body grows cold as the scene goes on, but the sisters don't mention him once. Not once. They chatter about tomorrow, about the music playing as the soldiers leave, about work, about whether people will think well of them in the future. They are passively responsible for their friend's death, because they never did anything to stop the duel. And what do they talk about? Anything but that.

When Konstantin Stanislavsky directed the first production of this play in 1901, he had an idea to parade Tusenbach's body around the stage at the end, presumably right under the sisters' noses as they talked and talked about anything but his death. Chekhov and the actors at the Moscow Art Theatre were horrified, and refused to let him drag a coffin around the stage. But Stanislavsky wanted to underline the fact that the most important thing in this scene is a shocking absence. He wanted to shove what is really going on in the audience's faces. In the last few minutes of the play, which are entirely about Tusenbach, the sisters are trying to make it about themselves. It is a violent act of exclusion.

It's useful to pay attention to what people quarantine. It takes effort to exclude something, and that often tells us even more about a character than the words they say. This can be tricky, because when something isn't there, we naturally tend to ignore it. The absent things are important. Our common-sense alarm bells should go off when we notice that a character is leaving something massive out.

Alex and Irina will find many life-giving things about the Macbeths when they imagine all the things the couple are keeping quarantined outside. Macbeth and Lady Macbeth have to struggle to keep all sorts of feelings at bay: the possibility of separation if they can't have another child; their grief about the dead baby; their fear that Macbeth will die in battle; the fear that they will fail. In every interaction they are trying to keep these feelings outside the scene. We all know what it is like to have unspoken things in the background of a relationship. Some couples have a nuclear button between them which they know they mustn't touch. Children especially have a knack of intuiting the things they must not mention.

Actors can find a living dynamic between their character and the rest of the world when they examine what they are trying to lock out. Whatever the character is trying to keep out of the space is often powerful and bangs at the door. That exclusion is never going to succeed permanently. The things that the Macbeths struggle to shut out batter on the door of their minds, putting pressure on the here and now, and heightening the stakes.

Struggling with these overwhelming outside forces pushing their way into the scene unlocks more life than can possibly be needed. Consequently, Irina and Alex need to search for the oceanic things outside that threaten to flood in and drown the character. This battle of inclusion and exclusion is just another type of fixing the space. It's the character's attempt to make the space feel safe and manageable.

◦— Characters quarantine space.

Alex is rehearsing Macbeth's soliloquy in the scene where the Macbeths are hosting a banquet for Duncan in the hours before they murder him. The pressure to keep up appearances has presumably become intolerable, and Macbeth deserts his wife at the table, leaving her to entertain the whole of the Scottish government by herself. He comes on stage to speak to us, the audience. He is torn in two. He is both terrified of doing the murder, and at the same time terrified of failing to do it. In the speech, he lists the pros and cons of killing Duncan, and finally seems to decide that the cons have it.

On the surface, it looks like a simple speech in which he changes his mind about the murder. But something else is going on here. As we have already discovered, we shouldn't necessarily swallow what the character tells us about themselves. No one speaks at such length without a reason. It's like an alcoholic telling you that they are not going to drink again. You feel happy for them. Then they give you a reason why. Then another. Fifteen reasons later, you start to worry. If they must give you so many reasons, it's because they have not yet convinced themselves. And we know that Macbeth hasn't managed to convince himself, because immediately following this speech it takes Lady Macbeth only a few seconds to put him back on track again. Here's Alex's text:

> *'If it were done when 'tis done, then 'twere well*
> *It were done quickly. If th'assassination*
> *Could trammel up the consequence, and catch*

With his surcease success; that but this blow
Might be the be-all and the end-all here,
But here, upon this bank and shoal of time,
We'd jump the life to come. But in these cases
We still have judgement here, that we but teach
Bloody instructions, which, being taught, return
To plague th'inventor. This even-handed justice
Commends th'ingredience of our poisoned chalice
To our own lips. He's here in double trust:
First, as I am his kinsman and his subject,
Strong both against the deed; then, as his host,
Who should against his murderer shut the door,
Not bear the knife myself. Besides, this Duncan
Hath borne his faculties so meek, hath been
So clear in his great office, that his virtues
Will plead like angels, trumpet-tongued, against
The deep damnation of his taking-off;
And pity, like a naked new-born babe,
Striding the blast, or heaven's cherubim, horsed
Upon the sightless couriers of the air,
Shall blow the horrid deed in every eye,
That tears shall drown the wind. I have no spur
To prick the sides of my intent, but only
Vaulting ambition, which o'erleaps itself
And falls on th'other...'

The first thing Alex will notice is that Macbeth talks to us as if we are his intimate friends. He chats to us as if we are old acquaintances. Except... we're not. There goes our common-sense alarm bell again. We don't really know this man. He certainly doesn't know us. But clearly, like all politicians, he needs something from us. If not our vote, then what? Maybe our reassurance? And again, like many politicians (and others), he tries to get what he needs by making us feel special.

The law of intimacy applies here as well. The only way he can include us as his friends is to exclude other people from this very special group. It would have been more natural to have this conversation with his wife – or Banquo, his best friend and companion in arms. But he's chosen us as his confidants. Notice that this special club only exists because there are people outside it. This is what Macbeth is doing in the first few lines. He is including us and excluding the people next door at the banquet. This kind of attention feels very flattering.

That's one of the things that Shakespeare does to us in each of the tragedies. The heroes or heroines address us directly and draw us into an intimate relationship. We feel privileged, and so, often despite ourselves, we warm to them. Too late, we realise that Shakespeare has chained us to a lunatic who's going to drag us through five acts of pure hell.

There is also another type of exclusion going on here. Macbeth is trying to control which thoughts and feelings are allowed to enter his space, and which he wants to keep locked out. This becomes obvious when Alex pays attention to what Macbeth is not saying. In Shakespeare, as in life, what is unsaid is often more important than what is said. Macbeth starts by saying to us:

> *'If it were done when 'tis done, then 'twere well*
> *It were done quickly.'*

Alex's common-sense alarm should be ringing wildly again. What on earth is Macbeth talking about? What does he mean by this 'it', a word he repeats four times in a line and a half? Well, Macbeth is planning to do something that will be a complete catastrophe for him, his family and his country. And somewhere deep down, he must know it. Of course he knows it. He is planning to murder the king. This is the entire topic of the speech.

If we listen carefully, however, we will see that he never actually utters the operative words 'murder' or 'king'. Three out of the four times this idea crops up in these first two lines, he uses the word 'it' instead. He is quarantining the essential words out of the speech. This should slap us awake. Macbeth doesn't want us, or indeed himself, to think too precisely about the most important thing, which is that he is planning a murder. A sordid killing of a kind old man who has given him a lot. As in addiction, he wants to do it before taking the time to consider what he is doing. Lady Macbeth feels the same in an earlier scene when she beseeches night to come,

> 'That my keen knife see not the wound it makes.'

Yes, this is delusional, but it's also very human. Macbeth doesn't want to take responsibility for what he plans to do. He must keep the shameful words out of the speech, as if by not saying them out loud, he's not really doing it. Instead, he uses the most impersonal word imaginable – 'it' – to avoid any clarity or emotion. He is presenting the murder plan almost as if he is showing us how to make an omelette. It's not a horrifying, grotesque murder. It's just an 'it'.

Later in this scene, both Macbeth and Lady Macbeth resort to increasingly ludicrous euphemisms to avoid saying 'murder the king', such as:

> *'his taking-off'*
> *'this business'*
> *'this terrible feat'*
> *'this enterprise'*
> *'the horrid deed'*

and (most preposterously)

> *'our great quell'*

Elaborate language is a defence against the facts. This flowery evasiveness is bullshit. It is disguised with perfume, but it is a stench we would do well to recognise. The Macbeths' increasingly overblown language reveals the amount of effort it takes for them to avoid saying the simple words 'murder' and 'king'. They even try to make the shabby little murder sound glamorous. Saying it clearly and simply would be unbearable.

This is an act of exclusion, but perfect exclusion proves an impossible goal. The more he blunders on with the speech, the more he fails to keep the door shut against the horrible reality of what he is about to do. He calls the murder an 'assassination'. Today, this is a word all too familiar to us, but to the play's first audience it would have sounded bizarre. In fact, this is the first recorded use of this word in English, and Shakespeare probably made it up. It would have sounded as odd to the first audience at the Globe as 'deathification' would to us. It's another flowery obfuscation of what is actually happening.

> *'If th'assassination could*
> *Trammel up the consequence, and catch*
> *With his surcease success.'*

What?! That's barely English! If you try to unpick it, the words *'catch with his surcease success'* might just about be stitched together to mean something like 'finish the job cleanly'. This is a spectacularly obscure way of saying something very simple. It's the kind of hokum the conjuror uses to distract while hiding the rabbit in the hat. All those sibilants in *'assassination'*, *'consequence'* and *'surcease success'* sound clever, but those whispery sounds just obscure the meaning even more. So is this bad writing on Shakespeare's part? No, quite the reverse. It is confusing speaking on

Macbeth's part. This mess of words is a deliberate choice. Shakespeare could write with devastating directness when he chose to.

As a great writer of humans, Shakespeare also had to be a master of bullshit. This is the sort of clever emptiness we use when trying to hide something. Again, it's exactly the way that politicians speak when they're talking to us about something unpalatable. When we are planning something unscrupulous, clarity is inconvenient. '*Surcease success*' is not brilliant poetry; it is an expression verging on nonsense.

As it comes out of his mouth, Macbeth can hear himself losing control of the words. He realises that we may be hearing him lose his grip. That only gives him another problem to fix. Now he must work even harder to convince us – and himself – that he's in control. He attempts to get back to a safe space by speaking in a long string of monosyllables. He uses simple, short words to attempt to put a straitjacket on his conversation with the audience.

> '...*that but this blow*
> *Might be the be-all and the end-all here,*
> *But here, upon this bank and shoal of time,*
> *We'd jump the life to come.*'

We should always pay attention when Shakespeare gives us a run of monosyllables: and here we get nearly four full lines of them. Here, they suggest a desperate act of verbal control. Macbeth is quarantining the space with simple monosyllables, trying to stop the mess and violence in his head from bursting out of his mouth. He can't afford to let us in the audience see the pandemonium inside. When he says:

> '...*that but this blow*
> *Might be the be-all and the end-all here...*'

it's as if wants this moment of the murder to be a time capsule that he can sever from the rest of his life. A moment out of real time. Macbeth imagines a version of the crime in which this moment is erased from his memory. Just like his wife, he is in an almighty battle to quarantine his feelings out of the space. He is in turmoil, but he doesn't want us to glimpse any of that chaos. He's trying to convince the audience that he is as cool as a cucumber. But he can't and he isn't.

This is a man who is way out of his depth, but who has given us an accidental glimpse of himself thrashing about helplessly. He has just run away from a dinner party. He was close to having a panic attack moments before the scene started, and the last thing he wants us to see is that he is spiralling wildly out of control. He wants to appear level-headed and logical, and in order to do that, he must shut out this brass band of doubt. He tries to quarantine the space by keeping the chat to practicalities and keeping feelings locked well outside it.

What he's really trying to do is keep the space safe, not just from the audience, but also from himself. He's trying to exclude the 'me' that he doesn't like: the 'me' who gets overwhelmed by his feelings and might chicken out at this chance at greatness; the 'me' who loves Duncan. This 'me' is a very inconvenient presence in Macbeth's space, one he is doing everything to shut out. Amputating a part of himself is one battle Macbeth can't win. None of us can.

To keep these waves of emotions shut out of the space, he tries to stick to pure, cool logic, and so now he goes off on a list of very sensible reasons he shouldn't commit the murder. He begins to sound like a barrister in a summing-up, appealing to the jury's common sense.

> '...*But in these cases*
> *We still have judgement here, that we but teach*
> *Bloody instructions, which, being taught, return*
> *To plague th'inventor. This even-handed justice*
> *Commends th'ingredience of our poisoned chalice*
> *To our own lips. He's here in double trust:*
> *First, as I am his kinsman and his subject,*
> *Strong both against the deed; then, as his host,*
> *Who should against his murderer shut the door,*
> *Not bear the knife myself. Besides, this Duncan*
> *Hath borne his faculties so meek, hath been*
> *So clear in his great office...*'

His legalese doesn't work. Even as he tries to list his thoughts calmly, uncontrollable images start crashing into his imagination. The longer he tries to lock his feelings out, the louder they batter on the door. Suddenly, outraged angels sweep down from above the stage:

> '...*that his virtues*
> *Will plead like angels, trumpet-tongued, against*
> *The deep damnation of his taking-off...*'

These angels paralyse his brisk, logical way of talking. His language starts to curdle, as if he has stepped out of the courtroom and right into the Book of Revelations. Suddenly, all those feelings of pity he has been working so hard to keep out smash down into the here and now in the shape of – yes – yet another baby:

> '*And pity, like a naked new-born babe,*
> *Striding the blast...*'

These ideas are smashing into Macbeth's space as powerfully as if they are real, flesh-and-blood beings. Macbeth does not control the ideas. They are not ideas. They are horribly concrete images that attack him physically. Alex's job is not to describe and convey the 'poetic' idea of trumpet-tongued angels or pity looking like a baby. His job is to see the naked, vulnerable baby as concretely as possible, as if it has just crashed through the ceiling. Like the knife in the earlier scene, the baby is a message from Macbeth's quarantined unconscious, shouting at him, 'This is mad, what you're doing is completely bloody mad, you don't even want to do it!' Mere theories of love vanish in the presence of a newborn baby. You don't need to be taught what love is when you look at an infant. It is the thing itself. The Macbeths know this all too well, because their dead baby haunts the castle. And the assaults from his imagination don't stop there. After the baby come more angels, but this time not outraged moralisers but Horsemen of the Apocalypse, crashing into Macbeth's space on blasts of wind.

> '…or heaven's cherubim, horsed
> Upon the sightless couriers of the air,
> Shall blow the horrid deed in every eye,
> That tears shall drown the wind.'

Macbeth couldn't be further away from the kind of measured control in the first line, when he started out with:

> 'If it were done when 'tis done…'

This is less like poetry, more like a fever dream. Fever, let's remember, is not a disease but the body's reaction to infection. These words are not a passive description of his thoughts. They are his sweaty, desperate reaction. Reaction to what? To a dreadful infection of feelings and images he is struggling and failing to lock out. The speech is a desperate attempt to make himself feel safe, a colossal battle between inclusion and exclusion.

THE OTHER SPACE

8

All scenes happen in the same place. This place is called 'here'. Every person and every character in every play is in their own version of this 'here'. Macbeth is in a chilly castle in Scotland, Rosalind is in the Forest of Arden, Viola finds herself on a beach in Illyria. You, wherever you are, are reading this book. I am now typing this on a laptop on a low coffee table. But these different places are called by the same name: 'here'. It's such a commonplace part of our second-to-second experience that we assume that here is, well… just here. But when we look closer, we notice something strange: all these different kinds of here have at least one other thing in common. They are all defined by things which are not here.

In fact, each 'here' has its own 'there'. 'Here' can't exist all by itself. It needs an opposite. For example, when I try to describe where I am right now, I can tell you it's cosy here, but that's probably because beyond the window it's raining. From that last sentence you might gather that I am inside, and so immediately know that I am not outside. When I tell you I'm upstairs, you become simultaneously aware that there is a downstairs. When I told you before that my laptop is on a low coffee table, perhaps you wondered why I'm not working (more sensibly) at a desk. The picture of 'here' is a jigsaw made up of opposite 'theres'.

Think of a Christmas TV advert selling traditional Yuletide cheer: Christmas trees, candles, a blazing fire, smiling grandparents, contented children. Often, the camera does not only show this scene. The shot may start with the snowy cold wastes of the garden, track past icicles on the windowpane, and only then show the cheery warmth of the family gathered around the fire. Someone inexperienced might think it a waste of time and resources to start outside, but the cleverer producer knows that they cannot make the illusion of warmth without first creating the illusion of cold.

Actors often ask a seemingly sensible question, 'Where am I?' They may think that if they can just pay attention to the here and now of the scene, their work will come to life. In fact 'here' cannot come to life all of itself, and much frustration and delay can result. Not only is 'there' equally important, but it must come *first*. Real energy never arrives alone at the press of some inner button. It needs two things to clash together to make a spark. At first, Alex might find this counter-intuitive, but the sandcastle can't exist without the ocean. And the ocean must come before the sandcastle. Alex needs to start by searching out what is over there. So what does the ocean over 'there' make happen for the 'here' of this scene?

✥ Look for what is over there that is making here dangerous.

Irina and Alex need to consider the scene next door. By 'next door', I mean a place on the other side of that wall, outside that door, or through that window. It has a specific location, which the character can usually point to. It is also always out of sight of the audience, but only just. And almost always, that scene next door defines what is going on in the scene in front of us.

Let's return to rehearsal with Alex, just after Macbeth has left the banquet. No sooner does Macbeth tell us that he has decided not to kill Duncan, than Lady Macbeth comes to find him. She is furious. He has abandoned her at the most important dinner party they have ever hosted in their lives.

MACBETH
> *How now! What news?*

LADY MACBETH
> *He has almost supped. Why have you left the chamber?*

MACBETH
>Hath he asked for me?

LADY MACBETH
>>>>Know you not he has?

MACBETH
>We will proceed no further in this business:
>He hath honoured me of late; and I have bought
>Golden opinions from all sorts of people,
>Which would be worn now in their newest gloss,
>Not cast aside so soon.

LADY MACBETH
>>>>Was the hope drunk
>Wherein you dressed yourself? Hath it slept since?
>And wakes it now, to look so green and pale
>At what it did so freely? From this time
>Such I account thy love. Art thou afeard
>To be the same in thine own act and valour
>As thou art in desire? Wouldst thou have that
>Which thou esteem'st the ornament of life,
>And live a coward in thine own esteem,
>Letting 'I dare not' wait upon 'I would',
>Like the poor cat i' th'adage?

MACBETH
>>>>Prithee, peace.
>I dare do all that may become a man;
>Who dares do more is none.

LADY MACBETH
>>>>What beast was't, then,
>That made you break this enterprise to me?
>When you durst do it, then you were a man;
>And, to be more than what you were, you would
>Be so much more the man. Nor time nor place

Did then adhere, and yet you would make both:
They have made themselves, and that their fitness now
Does unmake you. I have given suck, and know
How tender 'tis to love the babe that milks me:
I would, while it was smiling in my face,
Have plucked my nipple from his boneless gums,
And dashed the brains out, had I so sworn
As you have done to this.

MACBETH

                If we should fail?

LADY MACBETH
We fail?
But screw your courage to the sticking-place,
And we'll not fail. When Duncan is asleep –
Whereto the rather shall his day's hard journey
Soundly invite him – his two chamberlains
Will I with wine and wassail so convince,
That memory, the warder of the brain,
Shall be a fume, and the receipt of reason
A limbeck only. When in swinish sleep
Their drenched natures lie as in a death,
What cannot you and I perform upon
Th'unguarded Duncan? What not put upon
His spongy officers, who shall bear the guilt
Of our great quell?

MACBETH

             Bring forth men-children only;
For thy undaunted mettle should compose
Nothing but males. Will it not be received,
When we have marked with blood those sleepy two
Of his own chamber, and used their very daggers,
That they have done't?

LADY MACBETH
>Who dares receive it other,
>As we shall make our griefs and clamour roar
>Upon his death?

MACBETH
>I am settled, and bend up
>Each corporal agent to this terrible feat.

Alex and Irina may be tempted to start by exploring the dynamics of what is happening between Macbeth and Lady Macbeth. This is understandable. Isn't this what the scene is all about? Isn't this what the audience has paid good money to see? The psychological interplay is surely the most important thing to work on. However, this isn't the Macbeths' experience of this moment. For them, this scene in this room between the two of them is not half as important as the scene that is happening next door. It is a scene about Duncan, who is sitting between two empty chairs just on the other side of that wall. Embarrassingly, he has been abandoned by his hosts.

We can learn a lot by a simple act of subtraction. What would happen if there were no such scene next door? If Duncan wasn't sitting right there now in the next room, the Macbeths would be behaving in a completely different way. There would be no reason for this conversation to happen. Duncan is here in Glamis Castle, now, for one night only. Time and space have squeezed themselves into this one desperate chance, the chance to seize the moment. As far as the Macbeths are concerned, their onstage scene is only a footnote to what is going on next door. Without the next-door scene, this scene, this 'here', would have no reason to exist.

Duncan's presence doesn't just change the plot. His presence next door changes who the Macbeths are. They transform from inexpert pipe-dreamers into dangerous murderers, ravening for the blood of this kind old man who has been trusting enough to accept their hospitality. As a result, Alex and Irina must make Duncan and the banquet exist in their imaginations *before* they can start exploring what is happening between the Macbeths. This must happen first, because their relationship with each other here is completely dependent on it.

Sequence is crucial here. Alex and Irina cannot start building their onstage scene and then add next door afterwards as some afterthought. The space next door cannot be edited in later, like some CGI effect on a green screen. The actors must start building the other space first. They must start with what is next door.

⟶ The scene next door is more important than this one.

The devilish thing is that actors are always completely aware of the fact that Duncan is in the next room. There's no factual problem. Alex and Irina enthusiastically agree that Duncan's presence in the next room is important. But the problem does not lie in their understanding. Understanding only gets us so far. We can never 'understand' anything into life; Irina and Alex can never 'understand' Duncan into life, no matter how clever they are. If the presence of Duncan next door remains an idea rather than a concrete experience, then the scene cannot start to live. Life doesn't happen because we understand it. Life does not need permission from our intelligence.

Our job in rehearsal is always to turn ideas into experiences, and never the other way round. Exercises may help this. For example, it might be useful to stage the banquet using the rest of the company. This would allow Alex and Irina to experience what it actually feels like to push back their chairs, stand up, excuse themselves, and leave the table. It is a feast where the great and the good are assembled, celebrating a big victory, raising toasts, singing, perhaps shedding some patriotic tears. Alex and Irina might try the scene with all this noise coming through the wall, perhaps even with Duncan visible through a door.

All this is only to help Alex and Irina to experience the danger coming from the space next door, so that it is no longer a mere idea in their understanding, but instead an event that is happening in their bodies. They need to feel this event change their breathing, their heart rate, their sweat. The purpose of rehearsal is to remove an idea from the brain and put it into the body.

Locating the pressure from next door is crucial in all sorts of plays, even plays that appear to be all about onstage action. Let's think of the famous balcony scene in *Romeo and Juliet*. What is it about? Well... Romeo, and Juliet, and a balcony. But what is 'next door'? Well, just through the window, Juliet's parents are sleeping, and the Nurse is hunting around for her, calling out and threatening to wake the whole house up. On the other side of the orchard wall, the Montagues and Capulets roam the streets in the dark, searching for a fight. Security guards are just around the corner, patrolling the grounds. These places just next door radiate danger for this pair of teenagers. Should any of these forces burst into the scene, the fallout would be deadly. If it were somehow possible for Romeo and Juliet to meet, free from any pressure from next door, there would be no scene. In fact, it might just be that they would never fall in love in the first place.

The same situation is true of Chekhov's *Three Sisters*. The play's fuel comes from forces that are mostly absent from the stage. These include Moscow, the sisters' vanished youth, their dead father, their dead mother, and their lost hopes. Many of these unseen things are obvious, but there is also another particularly powerful 'next door' so obvious that it is sometimes overlooked: the small boring provincial town where they live, totally eclipsed in the text by the glamour of Moscow. In fact, their fantasy of Moscow takes up more space than the real town where they live. It is the imaginary place that allows them to feel superior to the local inhabitants. Being better than the town makes them feel special. In fact, their sense of existence depends on the fact that they are not part of this anonymous little backwater. They see themselves as temporary visitors, slumming it in the sticks.

At the end of the first act, one element of the town walks in. She's called Natasha, and it turns out that she's going to marry their brother, Andrei. The external pressure of the town has infiltrated the space, and that pressure drives the whole play forwards. She will fill the rooms with her children and gradually push the sisters out, like a cuckoo in a nest. By the third act, the pressure from the town increases. It is on fire just outside the window, and Vershinin's traumatised little girls are sobbing offstage at the bottom of the stairs, while the sisters themselves have taken refuge in a single bedroom above. By the end, Natasha and her lover, Protopopov, have taken over the whole house, and the sisters are driven out into the garden. The town has taken over. Next door has won.

The energy for so much of the play stems from this unconscious battle against the town, even though we never see the town on stage or even hear its name mentioned. It's always just out of sight, creating the conditions for most of the action. It's pressing through the walls of the house, dictating most of what they do. The sisters keep trying to exclude it, and to preserve the corner of time and space where they can feel superior. But just as with the sandcastle, it's a constantly losing battle.

Every scene in every play is the child of the scene next door. All the energy for any scene that an audience sees is being fed by this other invisible scene, as if through an umbilical cord. So if your work feels dead, why not look next door?

THRESHOLDS

9

Irina and Alex have now discovered that the Macbeths are obsessed with managing boundaries. They try to keep some things inside their space, and to keep other things well outside. They are constantly aware of the dividing line between this room and next door. They are hyper-attentive to the limits which separate their 'here' from their 'there'.

There is something magical about the boundary where one space becomes another. It is a crossing place full of change and danger. It is a 'threshold'. This has proved one of the most useful words in rehearsal. Humans are animals who are unusually preoccupied with thresholds. We go to the loo, and not only close but also lock the door. We are very careful about who is allowed to have our front-door keys.

Our fixation with thresholds is right there in the child's sandcastle. The children are choosing to play on the boundary between ocean and sand, the shifting line between solidity and destruction. On that massive threshold, they build little thresholds of their own, runnels and channels of water which create the boundaries of their vulnerable structure. It's a game about thresholds. And like many games, it is a rehearsal for the overwhelming processes of life.

We're not only obsessed with literal doorways, but with all kinds of crossing places. Across cultures and through time, humans have come up with all sorts of strange and intricate behaviours to mark rites of passage: baptisms and marriages, graduations and initiations, birthdays and funerals. Crossing places have a real power over our imaginations. As I get older, I have come to realise that it's never a good idea to miss a funeral. You must respect the power of a threshold. But thresholds are tricky to negotiate, even the simplest ones.

It's one of the important differences between making film and theatre. In a film, the director manages thresholds by cutting between scenes, and these choices are crucial. But in a play, you can't avoid the challenging problem of getting people on the stage and off it again. These entrances and exits are harder than one might think. They always require considerable thought.

What is a threshold? A threshold is where you move from one space to another. However, thresholds aren't just physical doorways. Think of a moment in which you are going to share something important: saying 'I love you' for the first time to a partner, for example. Whatever happens afterwards, as soon as those words are out of your mouth, you will be in a fundamentally different relationship. It will feel like you are in a new universe. Even if it proves a total anticlimax, that is still a threshold you have crossed.

Think about when someone new comes into the room. You must reorientate yourself around this new person, however minutely. We are always reading each other's status and shifting in reaction, even down to the smallest gestures and the way we angle our body. The entrance of the new person means your space has changed completely. It's as if you have suddenly found yourself in a different room altogether, with a new set of rules in it. Even though you haven't physically moved anywhere, you have still crossed a threshold. When we act any change, however tiny, it is useful to experience it as if we have passed through a kind of doorway into a new space. Crossing a threshold may not be easy. It may create friction, and therefore spark life. Every scene is a succession of thresholds.

- **Every change is a threshold.**

Interestingly, on the other side of every threshold lies exactly the same thing: that same thing is a surprise. We never find what we expect. Ever. The space never behaves exactly as we expect it to. Life is a continual surprise. The world can never behave precisely as we predict. As I look through my window right now, I notice that the sun has begun to stream through the rain. I have seen the sun fall across this table thousands of times, but it has never looked just like this, as it does today. And as I look up at the clouds outside, it makes me think that no one in history or space has ever seen these exact clouds. I can only see these shapes because I am looking at them from this spot, at this second, through these eyes. Everything is unpredictable, and therefore surprising.

While we are alive, everything is a surprise. Sometimes the surprise is a small one. But whatever the scale of the surprise, it pushes us, however slightly, to readjust ourselves, to change our position. One of the great things about dying is that there will be no more surprises. On the other hand, that is also the terrible thing about being dead.

Surprises make us uncomfortable because they remind us that we are not in control. We say we accept this, but I doubt we ever do, fully. We love to make plans to make ourselves feel safer, but unfortunately plans are nothing more than guidelines, hopes. They can never predict reality. Most wars start with an extraordinary number of plans, but all wars end up as horrific improvisations. Even if you plan something meticulously in advance, it never turns out quite as you intended. Let's think again about saying those loaded words 'I love you' for the first time. You may well have planned it for weeks, carefully engineered the perfect moment, but when you get round to crossing that threshold it, it is… well, *different*. And if something were to turn out exactly as you predicted, that should be the most colossal surprise of all.

◆― Crossing a threshold means meeting a surprise.

The surprise on the other side of every threshold is a source of life for the actor. It throws the character off track, however slightly. They are suspended in a moment of naked vulnerability as they work out how to deal with this new thing. The surprise on the other side of a threshold is a new problem the character must fix. It's a wonderful moment for the actor, because the character is out of control. Every time that happens, it is a tiny human epic. That moment of surprise teems with life. Every threshold is a gold mine for Alex and Irina. Remember: if the Macbeths are out of their depth, improvising, and trying to fix the space, then the scene is alive.

Surprise pumps at the heart of all acting. Inconveniently, it is also the actor's greatest challenge, because you cannot practise being surprised. You cannot package and commodify surprise. It must happen in the moment. Say you are decorating a film set and the scene needs a shot of a smashed egg. You could either: (a) spend a long time finding and consulting an egg-splatter expert, spreading out fragments of shell and yolk and egg white and arranging them in a believable spatter formation, and worrying whether the shell would fly further than the yolk or vice versa; or (b) chuck an egg at the floor. While (a) creates the more controlled image, (b) creates the more exciting image, because the outcome is out of your control. Your imagination (no matter how brilliant it is) can never execute something as alive as a real surprise. Your minutely prearranged egg-splatter will always be a little bit uncanny, a little bit dead. Over-preparation kills the surprise.

Showing surprise is not the same thing as letting yourself be surprised. In fact, it is the opposite. It's a great mystery at the heart of theatre – if you can't rehearse being surprised, how can you re-enact surprise at the right moment every night? There is no easy answer. No process can guarantee an alive and spontaneous performance, any more than training can ensure a football team always wins the match. The best thing the actor can do is give up trying to act and allow themselves to react to what they see.

It is for this reason that I find it impossible to answer when an actor asks, 'What is my character's attitude to this thing?' I can't tell you, because attitudes are unpredictable things. They are reactions, not things you generate. Surprise is one of those unpredictable reactions. So Alex and Irina can't precook being surprised every time they cross a threshold and then serve it up for the audience every night. As much as possible, they need to give up trying to control the entire performance. They need to be able to step on stage every night and see the Macbeths' world as if they are looking at changing clouds outside the window, discovering them anew each time. They need to be able to react as their instinct demands in the moment, not according to a predecided pattern.

In long runs of shows, inevitably a scene may start to become rote. That's when it is useful to intervene with a note to change it. The most useful notes are not new ideas, but about removing any extraneous structure that has crept into the performance by habit. However good that moment is, the attempt to replicate it perfectly is the pursuit of a dead thing. A living thing can never happen twice. In short, Alex and Irina need to prepare as much as possible in order to let go of as much as possible. They need to simply see and react. Only then will they find that life-giving moment of surprise on stage.

A good way to describe this moment of surprise is an encounter. In an encounter you see something for the first time. But, uncannily, it also seems to see you back. We don't just witness a surprise. We are changed by it. Crossing every threshold involves an encounter that changes you.

⌐ You cannot cross a threshold and remain the same.

The best way to describe an encounter is to think about what takes place when we look at a good painting. I love the paintings of Shakespeare's contemporary, Caravaggio. He took working men and women off the streets of Rome and turned them into biblical characters. His subjects have dirty feet and cracked toenails and scrawny sinews, but are all dressed up in draped sheets and gold-painted wigs and camp props. He plays with a discombobulating mixture of extreme realism and phoney kitsch.

When you stand in front of his canvases, the first thing that may strike you is, yes, his technical mastery, his balance of light and dark. But that's not what's great about Caravaggio. The longer you stand there, the more uneasy you feel. For the paintings seem to be looking back at you. They seem to be asking you what on earth you are doing, gawking at the Virgin Mary as she struggles to lift her child. Why are you here? What is your part in this? Caravaggio makes you question your right to be there. He throws you off-centre. Your encounter with the paintings changes you. They leave you in a much more ambivalent condition than when you came into the gallery to look at a piece of high art. They perform as a challenging mirror, forcing you to look back at yourself. This is, at the end of the day, what all good art does. An encounter exposes something at the heart of seeing. When we truly see, we are seen back. A true encounter leaves us momentarily exposed and vulnerable. Every encounter is a moment of jeopardy.

'Threshold' is also a useful word to ponder when we come to think about the act of thinking itself. We may imagine thought as a still, internal process. But thought is movement, movement in the space inside your head. For example, imagine a conversation in which someone says something offensive. In the sickening silence afterwards, your imagination bolts. '*My God, did he really say that?! – I could hit him! – Control yourself! – Does he expect me to agree with that? – What do I say next? – How can I get out of here?...*'

The experience of this moment is as if you're hurtling through rooms in your mind. Each thought feels like crossing a threshold into a new space. You find yourself in the middle of one thought and then you have a better idea, and it feels like you're wrenching open a door to another room and running into it. You arrive at a new thought, only to find it's useless, and you look for the next thought, slamming the door behind you on the last one. How many thresholds does your mind pass in those few seconds of silence? Too many to count. Our thoughts are distinct from each other. They are not like raspberry-ripple ice cream, with all the flavours running together into a pink sticky mess. They are spaces divided by walls.

Let's head back into the rehearsal room with Alex and Irina. They are still working on the end of the same scene from the last chapter, in which the Macbeths argue about whether to go ahead with their murderous plan. Let's consider it as a series of thresholds and see if that helps us. Pointing out the major thresholds in a scene is simply a useful key for unlocking life by giving us a basic structure to start work. It is not a recipe for the scene. Actors do not need to mark A,

B, C, D and E thresholds into their script and then try to hit the same points every performance. This is nothing more than a useful way of thinking when you get stuck, and a creative framework that encourages you to look for life in movement and space.

After Macbeth tells us about how conflicted he is, Lady Macbeth enters from the banquet. Every entrance is a massive threshold and presents many problems for a character to fix. The two spaces on each side of this doorway pressurise Lady Macbeth in different ways. On one side, she needs to perform as a gracious host, and on the other, she needs to fix her embarrassingly absent husband who is hiding in the room next door. That transition affects her whole body. It's a negotiation with the space.

Crossing the threshold changes her, changes every part of her body. And of course, what she finds on the other side is not what she expects. She's expecting to find her inept husband and bundle him back next door so they can continue their toasts. At the very least, she expects him to be apologetic for abandoning her at the most important dinner party they have ever thrown in their lives. But the surprise she encounters on the other side of the door is much worse than that. Macbeth is standing here, pale and sweating, refusing to move. He turns around and says to her,

'*We will proceed no further in this business.*'

To each of them this is a huge threshold. Lady Macbeth has walked in on a man she doesn't recognise any more. Surely the ambitious soldier she married could never be such a coward? A major ingredient in surprise is disbelief. Disbelief will help Irina hugely. When we cross a threshold in a high-stakes situation, we are not only surprised by what we find on the other side; we can't believe it.

Naturally the actor feels that their first problem is to believe. But often the situation is so extreme that the character cannot believe it. We only tend to believe things when the stakes are low. If Macbeth had told her he was just having a cigarette break, she may have been surprised, but could have believed him. But this is totally unthinkable. Did he just *say* that? Did he just break her trust?! Lady Macbeth is now profoundly out of control of the space. We can measure how vulnerable she must be feeling by the brutality with which she attacks. She mocks him:

> *'Was the hope drunk wherein you dressed yourself?'*

She humiliates him, calling him:

> *'A coward in thine own esteem.'*

She patronises him with babyish language:

> *'Letting "I dare not" wait upon "I would",*
> *Like the poor cat i' th'adage.'*

And she emasculates him:

> *'When you durst do it, then you were a man.'*

By now it's getting nasty. This isn't just a sexual taunt about his lack of potency. There is something else going on here as well, which is about him not growing up, about him being eternally a child. So long as he refuses to budge, she escalates. Each escalation is a threshold, a new, terrible, deadlier missile that changes the space between them. Macbeth can't believe what is happening either as she crosses these thresholds. He feels like he is desperately trying to keep up, to wrestle the space back into his control. And then she crosses the biggest threshold of them all. Out of nowhere, she says,

> *'I have given suck –'*

These words are like a bucket of ice.

> '– and know
> How tender 'tis to love the babe that milks me.'

Lady Macbeth has crossed a massive threshold. She has spoken the unspeakable, the thing they keep quarantined out of their relationship. She has brought their dead baby into the space. The baby they never talk about together, the baby whom we have already heard leaking into their thoughts. It's the loss of a baby they are grieving (or worse, perhaps, were never able to grieve). It seems to be something they have never recovered from, and understandably so. This dead baby haunts the play. A later scene includes the horrifying image of a dead baby whose body has been not only mangled, but dismembered, and the weird sisters are using its finger for their spell:

> 'Finger of birth-strangled babe.'

And here, Lady Macbeth doesn't just mention the baby. Like the witches, she mutilates it. She desecrates its memory in front of Macbeth's eyes.

> 'I would, while it was smiling in my face,
> Have plucked my nipple from its boneless gums,
> And dashed the brains out, had I so sworn
> As you have done to this.'

It's grotesquely shocking. That word '*boneless*' is so carnal. It is tactile because it is embedded in three-dimensional space. She relives the feeling of breastfeeding the baby, then murders it in front of Macbeth, like a sacrificial victim. It as if she's saying, 'I love you so much, we need to do this so much, do you know what I am giving up? Our baby. That's the blood sacrifice I offer up. I shit on our dead baby in front of you, *that's* how much this means to me.' She presses the nuclear button.

Lady Macbeth has brought them both across a threshold into a terrifying place. It's not just a threshold in the scene, it's a threshold in their marriage. Their relationship has different rules now. It exists in a new space, and they can never go back. After she's said it, it's not only Macbeth who can't believe what she has said. Neither can she. Did she really just dare to go that far? And as they both stand reeling in the debris of this devastating new space, the next unbelievable change happens. Out of the shell-shock, Macbeth asks,

> *'If we should fail?'*

That word 'we' is another monumental threshold. He has changed his mind. It's only the second time that word 'we' is spoken between them in the scene. The first time was when he sought to assert that '*We will proceed no further in this business*', but here it is truly inclusive. The first 'we' is always a big moment in any relationship. They are no longer in a fight between 'I' and 'you'. They are now in a 'we'. The universe has changed again. Relief floods the space for Lady Macbeth, and she replies:

> *'We fail?*
> *But screw your courage to the sticking-place,*
> *And we'll not fail.'*

In her triumphant echo of the word 'we', it's as if they have formed a mighty new organism together. They won't turn back now.

In short, the Macbeths experience this argument as if they are crossing boundaries between spaces. The space is changing wildly around both of them, faster than they can control, and hurling them into new territory at each twist and turn in the argument. Alex and Irina don't need to worry about how to make these twists and turns happen inside

Macbeth and Lady Macbeth. They need to think about them as changes happening in the space outside them. The scene is a series of dangerous thresholds – and the surprises they find on the other side.

TRYING OUT THE KEYS

10

Now we have a good handful of keys, let's pause for a moment and see how they might fit the lock. Here I want to issue a warning. This is not to suggest that Alex and Irina need to start rehearsal dutifully trying out all these keys at once. These keys are only for those times when we may feel stuck, locked in a room, lacking in energy, or feeling fake and unsafe.

Perhaps we might just use one of them, perhaps we might try several. We should remember that the point of a key is not to be clever or perfect or wise. The key is only there to unlock a door. If Alex and Irina aren't having trouble, they don't need a key. If they do need one, it's not always going to be predictable which one on the key ring will work. Maybe none will. Life offers no guarantees. These are nothing more than tools to keep in our back pocket.

In today's rehearsal, Alex and Irina are working on the scene directly following Duncan's murder. Lady Macbeth is waiting in the dark for her husband to creep down the stairs and tell her that he has killed the king. It should be their supreme moment. But, unfortunately, the instant Macbeth appears, everything unravels. He's hearing voices that seem to come out of the walls, and worst of all, he is still carrying the two daggers he was supposed to leave behind. She grabs them and takes them back into the room where the king lies dead, in order to incriminate his grooms.

LADY MACBETH
That which hath made them drunk, hath made me bold;
What hath quenched them, hath given me fire.
Hark! Peace!
It was the owl that shrieked, the fatal bellman,
Which gives the stern'st good-night. He is about it:
The doors are open; and the surfeited grooms

Do mock their charge with snores: I have drugged their possets,
That death and nature do contend about them
Whether they live or die.

MACBETH
Who's there? what, ho!

LADY MACBETH
Alack, I am afraid they have awaked,
And 'tis not done. The attempt and not the deed
Confounds us. Hark! I laid their daggers ready;
He could not miss 'em. Had he not resembled
My father as he slept, I had done't.

Enter MACBETH

My husband!

MACBETH
I have done the deed. Didst thou not hear a noise?

LADY MACBETH
I heard the owl scream, and the crickets cry.
Did not you speak?

MACBETH
When?

LADY MACBETH
Now.

MACBETH
As I descended?

LADY MACBETH
Ay.

MACBETH
Hark! Who lies i' th' second chamber?

LADY MACBETH
  Donalbain.

MACBETH
  This is a sorry sight.

LADY MACBETH
  A foolish thought, to say a sorry sight.

MACBETH
  There's one did laugh in's sleep,
  And one cried 'Murder!' that they did wake each other.
  I stood and heard them; but they did say their prayers,
  And addressed them again to sleep.

LADY MACBETH
  There are two lodged together.

MACBETH
  One cried 'God bless us!', and 'Amen' the other,
  As they had seen me with these hangman's hands.
  Listening their fear, I could not say 'Amen'
  When they did say 'God bless us!'

LADY MACBETH
  Consider it not so deeply.

MACBETH
  But wherefore could not I pronounce 'Amen'?
  I had most need of blessing, and 'Amen'
  Stuck in my throat.

LADY MACBETH
                These deeds must not be thought
  After these ways; so, it will make us mad.

MACBETH
  Methought I heard a voice cry 'Sleep no more!
  Macbeth does murder sleep': the innocent sleep,

Sleep that knits up the ravelled sleeve of care,
The death of each day's life, sore labour's bath,
Balm of hurt minds, great nature's second course,
Chief nourisher in life's feast –

LADY MACBETH

                                        What do you mean?

MACBETH

Still it cried 'Sleep no more!' to all the house;
'Glamis hath murdered sleep, and therefore Cawdor
Shall sleep no more; Macbeth shall sleep no more.'

LADY MACBETH

Who was it that thus cried? Why, worthy thane,
You do unbend your noble strength, to think
So brainsickly of things. Go, get some water,
And wash this filthy witness from your hand.
Why did you bring these daggers from the place?
They must lie there. Go, carry them, and smear
The sleepy grooms with blood.

MACBETH

                        I'll go no more:
I am afraid to think what I have done;
Look on't again, I dare not.

LADY MACBETH

                              Infirm of purpose!
Give me the daggers. The sleeping and the dead
Are but as pictures; 'tis the eye of childhood
That fears a painted devil. If he do bleed,
I'll gild the faces of the grooms withal,
For it must seem their guilt.

                                      Exit. Knocking within

MACBETH

                        Whence is that knocking?
How is't with me, when every noise appals me?
What hands are here? Ha! they pluck out mine eyes.
Will all great Neptune's ocean wash this blood
Clean from my hand? No, this my hand will rather
The multitudinous seas incarnadine,
Making the green one red.

                      Re-enter LADY MACBETH

LADY MACBETH

My hands are of your colour, but I shame
To wear a heart so white.

                              Knocking within

               I hear a knocking
At the south entry. Retire we to our chamber;
A little water clears us of this deed:
How easy is it then! Your constancy
Hath left you unattended.

                              Knocking within

              Hark! more knocking.
Get on your nightgown...

It is tempting to start by analysing the couple's psychology. Macbeth's extreme anxiety and Lady Macbeth's need to control her husband seem obvious at first sight. But as we know, in a rehearsal room it is not our job to play the armchair psychologist. There are humbler, and consequently much more useful, ways into the scene. Let's try a key in the lock.

◦— **Look for what is over there that is making here dangerous.**

'There' makes 'here' alive. And there are a huge number of dangerous 'theres' in this scene. So many that I count them differently every time. Here's a provisional list:

> Duncan's bedroom upstairs, where he lies in a pool of blood.
> The antechamber where the two servants are lodged together.
> An owl outside.
> Crickets outside.
> The place where Macbeth hears the first ghostly voice coming from when he's inside the bedroom.
> The place where Macbeth hears the second ghostly voice coming from.
> The staircase.
> The spot where Lady Macbeth left the daggers.
> The doors she left unlocked for Macbeth to open.
> The second bedroom, occupied by Duncan's son Donalbain.
> The Macbeths' bedroom.
> The bathroom where Lady Macbeth knows there will be water to wash with.
> The door at the south entry, where they hear the knocking.
> All the other bedrooms where the other guests are sleeping.
> The whole castle, which Macbeth thinks is echoing with these weird voices.

So far, this is a potential list of actual spaces around them in the castle. There are other imagined or remembered locations, which, as we have discovered, also feel real and concrete to the Macbeths. These include:

> The place where Lady Macbeth, as a child, saw her father sleeping (or perhaps even dead).
> The place where Lady Macbeth, as a child, saw a painting that looked like a devil.
> The sea, the only place where Macbeth thinks he can find enough water to clean the evidence of the crime from his hands.

You might have noticed something strange. If you go through this scene with a pencil and mark every time the Macbeths talk about a 'there', you will discover at least one in every single line. They are talking about almost anything except 'here'. Alex and Irina might reasonably think this is a scene between Macbeth and Lady Macbeth, but it isn't. This is a scene between Macbeth and Lady Macbeth exclusively about other places.

The Macbeths are instinctively avoiding being present with each other. They are focusing their attention on anywhere but here and any time but now. They think about the noise on the staircase, the owl outside, the knocking on the door, Donalbain's bedroom, the grooms... and on and on and on. They focus on any other place than here, on anyone else than each other.

Murdering Duncan was supposed to be their supreme moment, the consummation of their relationship, the ultimate coitus that will bind them together for ever. Earlier in the play, we heard them talk about it in airy euphemisms, dressing it up in poetic images. And indeed, if there were ever a moment when they ought to be present with each other, it is now. According to the self-deceptive rhetoric they have been spouting, this should be the very moment when they have proven to the universe that they are the chief agents of their own fate. They are seizing the opportunity life has dangled in front of them. They are the opposite of losers! They are triumphant! They will exist for ever!

But this is not what happens. As soon as they do the deed, they are slapped awake. They now must face the squalid reality of what they have done. They have slit the throat of an old man as he slept. It's messy and bloody and so horrifying to look at that neither of them wants to go into that room. They can no longer play the grotesque game of make-believe that murdering Duncan will be nothing more than an unfortunate collateral task on their path to greatness. They realise what in fact they had already known and were working so hard to deny. They have done an appalling thing, and it will stink for ever. Lady Macbeth desperately claims that '*a little water clears us of this deed*'. Really? In fact, their life will prove unbearable from now on. The one thing they thought would bring them together has blown them apart for ever. They can't bear to be present with each other. Instead, they turn their attention to anywhere else but 'here', and focus on a myriad of 'theres'.

Let's imagine what this scene would have looked like if everything had gone according to plan. Maybe it would go something like this:

> Macbeth slips out of the door and comes down the
>   stairs to meet his wife.
> They need no words, a thumbs-up will do.
> They embrace.
> They exit down the corridor.
> End of scene.

But this isn't at all what happens here. Why not? Because 'things over there' keep getting in the way of 'here'. Everything the Macbeths do in the scene are reactions to these 'theres'. Each one stops them from being the efficient murder team they had fantasised they were. Their entire experience of 'here' is now defined by those awful 'theres', which are hurling wildly different obstacles at them. They need to get to the safety of their bedroom fast, but things over there keep stopping them in their tracks. The ghostly voices, the spot where the daggers are supposed to be, the wakeful grooms, are all terrible and unexpected problems they must deal with. Their impulses are torn in two. As much as they want to run away, they have obstacles they have to scramble over.

In short, for the Macbeths, or any character, life is problem-solving. Find a problem over 'there', and the scene comes to life. When there are no problems, the scene is either dead or, like the description above, amazingly short. Fortunately for Alex and Irina, there is a wealth of 'theres' making here dangerous. Donalbain's bedroom, the guards' bedroom, the castle full of sleeping guests, are all places vibrating with the possibility that someone will wake up. Every one of the Macbeths' senses is dialled up to eleven, tuned into these other spaces. Shakespeare understands so well that when the stakes go up, we become acutely conscious of the space. In their panic, the Macbeths become hyper-vigilant, scanning for the dangers around, real or imagined.

Pointing out all these 'theres' is not a clever psychoanalysis of the scene. The aim is to help Alex and Irina get out of their heads and into their bodies. They will soon notice that these other locations are pushing and pulling the Macbeths through the scene like magnets. They feel utterly compelled to get to their bedroom over there, but the problem of planting the daggers over *there* pulls them in the other direction. Macbeth wants to run far, far away from Duncan's bedroom right over there, but the disembodied voices coming from over *there* are a terrifying problem he needs to solve first in order to keep his grip on reality. Also, in all this rush and panic, they need to move silently and make sure they don't rouse Donalbain, asleep behind the door there, but the knocking on the south entry over at yet another there means they need to escape to their bedroom fast.

Now, to draw as much energy as possible from these powerful 'theres', Alex and Irina need to make sure they aren't vague. They need specific locations, and they must be able to picture them vividly. The owl can't be 'sort-of-over-there'. It needs to be *exactly* there. Donalbain's bedroom needs to be an actual place they can point to, however fleetingly. Lady Macbeth's memory of her sleeping father cannot be a hazy idea. She needs to be able to see the spit dribbling out of the corner of his mouth. Specificity gives these dangerous things-over-there power and life. And this is the only source of life-giving energy that the actor can rely on.

All these dangers over 'there' pressurise the way the Macbeths move 'here', and change what they can do with their voices, where they are standing, the tension in their muscles. Their whole bodies react to the dangerous environment, pressurised by 'theres'. They believe they can dominate the space, but the space dominates them. All their behaviour is a reaction to threats around them. Nothing goes the way they want it to in this scene. Reality is just not what they want it to be. They can't control the space. They can't even control their own imaginations, which torture them with memories and hallucinations at the very moment they need to stay clear-headed. This will help Alex and Irina, because they don't have to feel like they are making things happen. Things are already happening, and all they need to do is respond.

⌁ The scene next door is more important than this one.

Of all the 'theres' the Macbeths talk about in this scene, one is more powerful than all the others. It's the room, just up those stairs, where Duncan lies in a widening pool of blood. To the Macbeths, that scene upstairs is far more important than this space here, where they are speaking to each other. What has happened in that room is so awful that it changes their experience of reality for the rest of their lives. When Macbeth comes out and speaks to his wife, his imagination is still nailed to the room where he did that unseeable thing. He's in one space with Lady Macbeth here, but overwhelmed by this other space upstairs there. He has seen the blood-soaked bedroom, but she hasn't. Macbeth's mind is now stuck in that room next door for ever, and it will haunt him for the rest of his life. He can't be fully present anywhere else ever again.

It becomes a hypnotic space for Lady Macbeth too. Once she opens the door of that room, she can no longer see the airy theory of her '*great quell*'. Instead, she sees the waxy skin of the butchered old man who looks like her father. She will never be able to leave that room again either. From here on in the play, they both descend into full, stomach-churning paranoia. From this moment on, there will be a threat shifting behind every door. From this moment on, there will be no safe space called home. They will only exist in corners and corridors, trying to build imaginary safe spaces inside their heads. Even there, they can't feel safe, because witches and daggers and angels and ghost babies and God knows what keep bursting in to torture them.

Let's try another key.

◦— The space is always in flux.

The space never stops giving the characters problems to solve. This evolving threat provides a constant source of life to the actors, even as it slowly murders the Macbeths. Let's have a look at Lady Macbeth's speech right at the start of the scene, and see how this might help Irina. Like every character in every scene, Lady Macbeth is fighting to create a little patch of control for herself. Just a little corner of time and space. But every time Lady Macbeth thinks she's sorted, the space changes and throws her off balance again.

When the scene starts, Lady Macbeth is in a corridor in the dark, waiting for Macbeth to kill Duncan. Waiting is always hell, but she is not waiting alone. Of course, the audience is in the space as well. She sees us staring at her, expecting her to do something. This puts pressure on her, so she brags:

'That which hath made them drunk, hath made me bold;
What hath quenched them, hath given me fire.'

As we have seen, every soliloquy is a conversation with the audience, a series of replies to what the character thinks the audience is thinking. Perhaps Lady Macbeth sees a silent judgement in our eyes: what is she doing skulking around the corridor like a coward when she should be helping her husband murder Duncan? She speaks to correct our opinion. She's terrified, and so she needs to persuade us that she's not. 'No!' she's saying. 'I'm a criminal mastermind!' Unfortunately, the space keeps undermining her. A second later, a sudden noise makes her jump out of her skin, giving the lie to all her bravado.

'Hark! Peace!'

The space has changed. It has refused to remain neutral and easy to deal with. It's behaving like a haunted-house fairground ride, full of startles and shocks. And as soon as she's jumped out of her skin, Lady Macbeth looks at the audience, and sees a new problem in our eyes. We have just witnessed her freak out. Now she must work even harder to convince us that she is cool and calm and unflappable. She does so with a poetic image about how the owl is yet another example of the world being on her side. She tells us this owl brings bad luck for Duncan, not for her.

> *'It was the owl that shrieked, the fatal bellman,*
> *Which gives the stern'st good-night.'*

Hardly convincing. She can see her failure in the audience's eyes. She's lost that round, and so she tries a different tack.

> *'He is about it…'*

Now it's as if she's saying, 'Okay, maybe you just saw me lose my cool, but my husband's sticking the knife in right now, on my instructions. I've got it all sorted. I'm in control.' She goes on to persuade us how brilliantly she has orchestrated the plot:

> *'The doors are open; and the surfeited grooms*
> *Do mock their charge with snores: I have drugged their*
>   *possets,*
> *That death and nature do contend about them*
> *Whether they live or die.'*

She's boasting that even sleep and death are at her command. She brags that she can control nature. A few scenes ago, we heard her tell Macbeth that even time was her servant, when she claimed to see *'the future in the instant'*. All these ludicrous boasts are a symptom of her desperation to convince herself and us that she remains in perfect control. But the irony is that sleep, death and time will undo her all too soon.

Once again, whenever she looks at the audience they never seem fully convinced, so she blusters on like a frightened eleven-year-old. Lady Macbeth is in a battle with the audience that she can never win – and this is good news for Irina. Then, suddenly, she hears Macbeth shout. The space changes yet again. Her mask slips and that hidden terror leaps out again uncontrolled:

'Alack, I am afraid they have awaked...'

...and so on and so on. This constantly changing space is the pattern for this scene, and indeed for all scenes. Wave upon wave engulfs the sandcastle. Every time Macbeth and Lady Macbeth think they have got their space under control, it changes again, and they struggle to keep up. Their space is always unpredictable and refuses to behave as they want. Macbeth thinks the murder is over and done with, and then voices start coming out of the walls. Lady Macbeth thinks that the murder is over and done with, and then realises Macbeth has brought the daggers out of the bedroom with him. The Macbeths think they are the only ones awake, and then there is a knock at the south entry. Their characters can barely solve one problem before the space hurls another one at them.

Another key:

> **The space isn't just outside us. It's also inside our heads.**

Alex and Irina need to be in the exhilarating position of reacting to things, and not in the hellish prison where they need to generate things inside. To do this, they may need to redraw that frontier between internal and external, and imagine as many things as possible live in the outside world.

Emotions

This is a scene where emotions run high. However, Alex and Irina can't summon their feelings from inside. For example, Lady Macbeth doesn't experience her fear as an internal state. To her, it seems her fear attacks her from the space. The owl hoots. The thought crashes into her brain that Macbeth can't find the daggers in the dark. She hears Macbeth shouting and waking up the house. All these things frighten her. They are arrows of fear firing at her, into her, not fear that exists inside her. She gets attacked by her fear, she reacts to her fear, she tries to manage her fear. And this will give Irina much more energy than somehow trying to generate fear internally.

Memories

Memories attack Lady Macbeth continuously throughout the scene. They haunt her, paralyse and startle her. They tend to rear their heads exactly when she doesn't want them. Lady Macbeth could have plunged the knife into Duncan's flesh, if only the memory of her sleeping father didn't get in the way. And these memories keep invading. She cannot lock them out. Later in the scene, she scoffs at her husband:

> *'tis the eye of childhood*
> *That fears a painted devil.'*

But this image of the painted devil has all the vitality and intimacy of something she has experienced personally. We imagine the wide-eyed little girl, staring at a pattern that seems to represent a nightmarish devil. She mocks her husband for behaving like a child, but in doing so we glimpse her own childish fragility. It's another moment when she is trying to keep her panic locked outside the door, but without success.

Macbeth too is tortured by memory, but one very recently formed – that of watching his own fingers kill Duncan. The remembered image keeps invading his head like a fever dream. The memory is so violent it stops him from going back into that room.

'Look on't again, I dare not.'

It is as if the memory has entered his body and changed his DNA. The trauma is there in the strange sense of dissociation from himself. He hears voices talking about himself in the third person, as if he is adrift from his own body. He starts talking about his hands as if they belong to someone else. He calls them *'a sorry sight'* to Lady Macbeth, and later turns to us to ask, *'What hands are here?'* His own bloody hands must belong to someone else… some guilty person. Logically, of course, he knows they are covered in blood. He's just stabbed a man to death. But we humans are not always logical creatures. He has a strange sensation that he doesn't recognise his own hands or understand why they are dripping with blood. Every time he looks down at them, the memory of what he has just done attacks him with such force that his mind runs away and refuses to believe his body belongs to him. Someone else must have done it. And he talks and talks and talks. As often, talk swaps responsibility for bullshit. Clearly, both the Macbeths experience memories in this scene as physical forces attacking them from the space, not as internal thoughts. The truth is that they are internal thoughts, but that is of absolutely no use to the actor. It is just not how experience works.

Ideas

As we noticed in an earlier chapter, the idea called 'Murdering Duncan' seemed to take flesh and live with them as a third person in the Macbeths' marriage. Remarkably, they are still using euphemisms like '*it*' and '*the deed*'. Only other people, like the waking grooms and the mystery voice, use the word 'murder'. Neither of the Macbeths can bring themselves to take responsibility for the word, never mind the deed. The word itself is so big, so powerful, and so out of their control that they can't bear to utter it, except when reporting someone else's speech.

Me

Lady Macbeth also has a problem with herself. She doesn't like 'me'. This inadequate 'me' let her down when she couldn't stick the knife into Duncan herself. So, in the hope that she will transform into her, she promotes a fake version of herself. Her 'me' is another problem she must solve in the space. As we have already noticed, Macbeth also becomes increasingly disconnected from his own version of 'me' throughout the scene. Soon he can't recognise himself any more.

Or this key:

⚯ **Characters quarantine space.**

As we have now seen, both Macbeths are experiencing an onslaught of powerful emotions like guilt, doubt, fear and panic, which they are constantly struggling to exclude. When Macbeth calls the murder '*a sorry sight*', he accidentally lets his pity and remorse off the leash, and they slip into the space. Lady Macbeth counters with a scoff – '*A foolish thought, to say a sorry sight*' – slamming the door on these inconvenient feelings. Her reaction is swift and brutal. She wants to strip the scene clean of remorse. This struggle dominates every line. She is trying to cordon off Macbeth's feelings, and indeed quarantine her own. They do not experience this as an abstract concept but an almost physical process of pushing things outside in order to keep themselves feeling safe inside. This struggle should be felt in their bodies. It's a carnal battle for survival.

Lady Macbeth must use every weapon at her disposal, every gram of scorn she can muster, to exclude any possibility of failure. She has never seen her husband's face look exactly like this before. She sees his body buckling under the strain and struggles to put him back together again. She uses a fraught combination of mockery, cajoling, bullying and mothering. She must lock out the slightest remorse, doubt, weakness, disappointment or dread of loss.

For Alex, it may be helpful to think that in every line, Macbeth is struggling to exclude his sense of imminent catastrophe and at all costs to keep chaos at bay. Once again, for each actor, this is all about the space. It's about trying to carve out and quarantine a space within which they might feel safe. And when it doesn't work, they must try again. Of course, they will never achieve it. They will never find a space in which they are safe.

The actor should never have to power up the scene, never have to manufacture the action. These are unnecessary and fake responsibilities that will overwhelm the actor. Only the space can feed them what they need. The chief difference between the character and the actor is that the space is the character's enemy but the actor's friend. This will keep the two usefully divided.

As said repeatedly, Alex and Irina should never see these keys as rules. However, any one of them might just open that troublesome lock and release a flood of life-giving energy.

FLOW

11

Life in the space depends on the flow between the actors, and it follows that at the start of rehearsals we need to establish a space in which the actors can find flow. Now, while it's impossible to define exactly what 'flow' is, it's another one of those important things that becomes painfully apparent when it's absent. Without flow, bodies freeze, and actors become fatally self-conscious.

Flow is something to do with finding yourself instinctively reacting without second-guessing. Flow is an open channel of receiving information from outside and reacting freely. Your body knows what to do, without any orders from your brain. Anyone in team sports knows what flow feels like. If you watch football from ground level, each player looks like they are doing their own independent task – but they are not. When the camera shows us a bird's-eye shot from above, we can see that they form an improvised pattern, a sort of dance. A tiny dart one way from one midfielder causes another on the other side of the pitch to adjust their position in response, keeping a flexible diamond moving up and down the field. The players will know when they are in flow, as they use every one of their senses and their maximum peripheral vision to keep track of each other. They have given over their bodies to a process of pure reaction which short-cuts any instruction from their conscious minds. This is one of the most exhilarating experiences they will have.

Flow is precious and invisible. If we look up at a flight of starlings we witness a powerful mystery, almost a miracle. They seem to have no leader, and yet the flock, the 'murmuration', changes direction instantaneously and perfectly. They don't argue and never bump into each other! Many cultures have been so overwhelmed with this evidence of flow, that the flight of birds became a central augury to be interpreted by priests.

Flow underpins everything we do in rehearsal. The most vital performances are the ones in which all the actors, in every moment, are participating together in a give-and-take: a living, breathing flow. They each have very different parts to play, but they are still equal in this flow. And this flow feeds them.

◈— **Attend to the flow.**

Unfortunately, there is no formula on how to achieve flow. It is a delicate ecosystem that feeds and is fed by everyone, and it's up to all of us in the room to make sure that it is a space open to flow. Like life, you can only create the conditions for flow, not make flow itself. This is one reason why it can be dangerous to let visitors observe rehearsals. Even if they sit silently in the corner, they will affect the ecosystem. At the beginning of rehearsals, the flow in the room is normally appalling. The company is naturally anxious, and communications with each other can be quite staccato. Tense laughter makes it even worse. We can't force flow to happen, however much we might want to. At the start of a sticky party, we sometimes throw ourselves at the alcohol to 'loosen up'. It can seem to work, but...

So, if we can't make flow, let's see if we can remove things that might block it, anything that tends to stifle the actors' natural impulses and movement. For example, we have found that reading the script around a table on the first day can be counterproductive. Flow is born out of movement, so we may start with children's games, which give the actors permission to move and connect with each other, with nothing at stake. We will learn a song and a dance, with no expectation that they will be used in the production. They serve the simple but crucial purpose of getting the actors moving in the space together as a company.

If we can achieve flow, we will be able later to harvest the images born organically. With the right atmosphere, extraordinary things appear of their own accord. And, conversely, any precooked ideas that we came into the rehearsal room with are blown away like dead leaves. Astonishingly, we may discover how little new information we need. As often, the problem is not too little but too much information.

However, a warning: if we talk about flow or analyse it too much, it dies. We must have a light touch, and open the channels to an atmosphere of attentiveness and generosity with each other and our own imaginations. Flow is about the actors' openness to the space, their ability and willingness to give up some control and react. They need to risk letting the space make some decisions for them. In short, we're not attending to an outcome, we're attending to the flow. It's not about result; it's about process. Find the flow, and the results will tend to take care of themselves.

It can be dangerously tempting to think of honing a performance as if you are creating some complex and self-sufficient object like, say, a Fabergé egg. As if the goal is to win the audience's admiration with our dazzling perfection. But there's a problem with a Fabergé egg. It never changes. It's a dead thing, like a sandcastle built up on the dry sand. Instead, let's search for flow. Out of it, life will spring in all its unpredictable, maddening glory.

That said, there is a caveat: we should not entirely surrender ourselves to flow. Actors should not erase themselves and become entirely subsumed to some collective. Actors need flow with each other to create life, but they also need to retain their individual responsibility. Flow without responsibility is very dangerous. There is a reason that, throughout history, soldiers have been drilled to march in unison. On one hand, how much individual responsibility do we each have to keep? And on the other, to what extent must we give up control to the group? The answer is: just enough. And the only way to judge that is by using your common sense and developing it through experience.

Once flow is established, rehearsal has a very specific purpose. It becomes all about investigating the experiences present in the script and making specific discoveries. Take one of the first scenes in *Macbeth*, where Macbeth and Banquo are trudging across the Scottish countryside after a battle. We need to investigate what it's like to be on the heath, what it's like to be hungry, what it's like to be cold, what it's like to be slogging through the rain, what it's like wanting to get home. We will do all that on our feet, moving, in flow we hope, with minimal discussion.

This is an example of what we call the 'invisible work'. It gives us the imaginative structure we need for the performance to happen. The invisible work includes all sorts of different things. It may involve deciding where the major thresholds are, and on the changes the space goes through. It might involve exploring some of the major experiences that have shaped these characters' lives, like the loss of the Macbeths' baby, or the battle that happened just before the play began. We have found it's best to explore these things through movement and flow, and with as little analysis or improvised words as possible. Every theatre-maker will develop something that works for them. The invisible work is all the preparation we must do as a company that the audience never gets to see – and indeed must never see. But the second Irina and Alex step on stage to perform, they must forget about it.

'What?!' ask Irina and Alex.

Yes. If the actors try to hold on to all this preparation in their heads, they will have no freedom to react to the space. Instead, Alex and Irina need to have faith that all their invisible work will be waiting, ready to jump out and feed the life of the scene. It's like a pianist who practises the music repeatedly, so they can trust that the memory is in their fingers when they are ready to play a concert. The concert will be deathly if the pianist is going through it only thinking about executing the next note. They must let themselves go, trust in their preparation, and just... play.

The precise reason for learning things is so we can forget them. If they are important things, well learned, they will stick around on your mental hard drive. When you wander near a cliff edge, on the whole you don't need to remember how dangerous it is. It remembers itself. You can't play the invisible work. The invisible work plays you. It would be a dead performance if the audience was watching the actor remembering things from rehearsal. An actor's lines need to come automatically for the character to invent them in the moment.

But, of course, there are elements of a performance that we can't avoid controlling. Fight scenes, the timings of entrances and exits, the rough location of the action on stage – all these need to be structured to a certain extent in order to keep the company safe and the story legible. However, these are just anchors that give us the confidence to allow flow. We need some structure but also need to make sure it is as minimal as possible. No structure equals chaos, but too much structure can suffocate us. Rehearsing is like building a climbing frame that invites the actors to negotiate it slightly differently in every performance.

If you try to remember all your invisible work, you will overfill your head and feel blocked. Søren Kierkegaard used an unsettling image of a man who is dying of starvation because his mouth is so full, he can't swallow. How do you keep him nourished? The only way to feed him is first to take food *out* of his mouth.

> **You can't let anything new into your brain until you make space for it.**

The same is true for a director. We need to prepare well before rehearsals so our heads can be empty when the actors walk in. The preparation won't have disappeared. We can trust that it is there on the back-burner. The most important thing is that we need to be able to see what is happening before us and respond. This is a surprisingly hard thing to do. Any directorial ideas or fantasies we have cooked up in advance may blind us to what is happening between the bodies before us. We need to see what is happening now, in this tiny corner of time and space. This is a lifetime's struggle. Opening yourself up to flow involves a leap of faith. You must trust yourself and the people around you enough to give up some control. It may feel unsettling – but it's also the only narrow strip of shore where life can take place.

CHARACTER

12

Let's question another 'friend' that might be blocking flow. This is the idea of building a character. Phrases like 'getting into character', 'working on a character', and 'getting to the heart of a character's truth' are often heard. 'Get' is an idea deeply rooted in English, in such phrases as 'get some attention' or 'get lucky'. The idea of 'getting' implies there is a thing that can somehow be possessed. When it comes to a character, there isn't. For, effectively, there is no fixed central truth to a character.

We behave differently around lovers, strangers and colleagues, whether we are on the bus, in a bar, or on the beach. We perform different versions of ourselves at different moments. We all know how vulnerable we feel when we introduce a new partner to our family, or a childhood friend to a colleague at work. One of the reasons is because we become aware that each sees different versions of us colliding in that moment. However, neither of these versions is false. Each is an equally valid part of ourselves. We need to be quite comfortable with slipping from one role to another. We shouldn't fall for the fantasy that we have the duty, or indeed the right, to be just one thing, and that we are deceiving ourselves if we are not. If we feel we ought to be one thing, we will prove as unstable as a stool with only two legs.

Attachment to character is understandable. Given all the uncertainty involved in acting, the idea of having a character to hold on to is a comforting one. But this involves the assumption that a character is a thing that will behave predictably. This is neither true nor useful. Everything, remember, is in flux. That includes our characters. We are not who we were an hour ago. The problem is that we have become wedded to ideas, often virtues, like 'authenticity'. It is very tempting to think that there is a monumental fixity at the centre of our characters, an essence of me, that never changes and therefore makes me feel safe and good and always in control.

Macbeth suffers from this fantasy. The very first time in the play that he speaks to the audience, he has just heard the witches' prophecy. It sends him into a spin. He says:

> *'Present fears*
> *Are less than horrible imaginings.*
> *My thought, whose murder yet is but fantastical,*
> *Shakes so my single state of man that function*
> *Is smothered in surmise, and nothing is*
> *But what is not.'*

In this tremendous run of words, we can easily miss a deadly idea lurking inside: *'my single state of man'*. A problem underlying Macbeth's terror is that he feels he has the right to be one thing, a single state. He imagines that he has an essential, authentic 'Macbeth-ness' that defines him. It is a very comforting delusion, and we hear it again later in the play, when Macbeth tries to cover his tracks by murdering Duncan's sleeping grooms before they can incriminate him. Macduff asks why he killed them without having questioned them first. Macbeth lies by claiming that, in the moment, his fury overtook his judgement. He says:

> *'Who can be wise, amazed, temperate and furious,*
> *Loyal and neutral, in a moment? No man.'*

He's wrong again. The answer should be 'Every man'. We are all full of illogical contradictions. Being a human is complicated. It is scary to admit that the character we find the hardest to understand is ourselves. We don't really know who we are.

How many times have you asked yourself, 'Why the hell did I do that?' None of us fully knows what we are capable of.

Some versions of the Lord's Prayer include the words, 'Do not put us to the test.' This phrasing understands that we are all frail. It acknowledges that morally, ethically, as human beings, we do not know what we might do or indeed who we are, until we are tested. We don't know who we are until we come into conflict with the space. We don't know how we are going to react until we reach the moment itself, especially when the stakes are high. None of us knows who we might become in an extreme situation.

It's a hard lesson, and Macbeth learns it horribly. He doesn't recognise himself after Duncan's murder. He had always considered himself to be a professional soldier, professionally desensitised to violence. He was a man who, days beforehand, disembowelled and decapitated a man on the battlefield. We are told that he *'unseamed him from the nave to the chops'*, all without a second thought. But today is another day, another him. Today he finds his hands dripping with Duncan's blood. And he discovers that, amazingly, this blood is not like any other blood. He's shocked that this blood shocks him. He discovers another Macbeth, a Macbeth with feelings that he didn't know existed.

One of the reasons it's difficult to get rid of our attachment to authenticity is because advertising sells it to us all the time. Advertisers want us to think that there is an authentic version of ourselves; that if you buy a product, it will get you a little bit closer to the wonderful essence of the true you. This aftershave will release the tiger in your tank; this bank account will help you have the happy family you deserve; this shampoo will reveal your natural beauty to the world. Populist leaders often tell you that there is an immutable part of you that is somehow rooted in the soil of your country. If we entitle ourselves to the delusory right to be just one thing, we make ourselves susceptible to all these persuasions. The concept of authenticity can be dangerous. Better to accept the fact that our 'self' is constantly shifting, beautifully unstable and endlessly unpredictable.

So, what if we stop talking about a character as a 'thing' we can 'get'? What if we demote the very idea of a character? What if we jettison 'getting into character' from our rehearsal to-do list? Let's drop the baggage of assuming we must sweat away getting to the heart of some authentic truth about a character. Alex and Irina can ditch the daunting idea that their task is to construct some sort of character, which they then invite the audience to sit down and admire. Their Fabergé egg might impress at first glance, but it will be an unchanging thing that can only be dead. It is nothing like the great boiling pot of contradictions that make up a living human being. For all their many talents, the one thing Alex and Irina cannot do is fashion a character all by themselves. No actor can. It's impossible. What they can do is rely on the space to do the job for them.

⚜ Only the space can bring the character into life.

Our context defines who we are. We are defined by the time and space we find ourselves in. You can't take people out of their context and imagine that their character would be the same. If Shakespeare lived now, he would not be Shakespeare. He might not even be a playwright at all. He bought the second-best house in Stratford. It would be awful if we transposed him to the present day, just to find out that he only wanted to talk about Warwickshire property prices. It is more useful to imagine that our characters only come into existence when we interrelate with our space. When we cease to interact with the space, our characters disappear.

Let me put this another way. What is the space? It's what gets taken away from us when we die. What is death? It's what happens to us when the space gets taken away. My life, my alive-ness, is not a state. It is a constant process of interaction with the space. I am alive right now because I am breathing in air. I am seeing a pigeon on the windowsill. I am listening to the bus outside. I am trying to connect with you across a vast distance, trying to imagine whatever you might be thinking about these words, whoever you might be. I am alive right now because I am interacting with the space. Life is woven into the space.

When someone dies you lose not only them, but also the space that existed around them. We may think we miss the essence of that person, but in fact we miss the way they interacted with the space: the way their face lit up when they saw you; their fearful swearing when they got overtaken by another car; the way they sneaked a surreptitious cigarette hoping you wouldn't notice. And most particularly, you miss the way they smiled at you. They take with them what they saw when they looked at you. So, when they die, that part of you dies as well, the version of you that lived in their eyes.

It's their relationship to the world that we miss, because that is them. We miss the space they leave behind. In *Tom and Jerry* cartoons, you often see Tom run through a door, comically leaving a precise cat-shaped hole behind him. But this is precisely what death is *not* like. We don't just leave our empty outline behind us. We take our whole universe with us as well.

You cannot detach a person's life from the space. The Venerable Bede, an eighth-century Anglo-Saxon writer, gave a marvellous definition of life. He said it's like a bird at night that flies into a feasting hall. It flies out of darkness into the light of the hall, and then out through another window into darkness again. You don't know where it is coming from, you don't know where it is going, but it is illuminated for the few seconds it crosses the room. It is an image that can help us think about how life depends on the space.

Characters depend exclusively on their relationship with things outside them. Even a hermit in retreat from the world will have a relationship with the god they worship, the air they breathe, the food they eat, and indeed with their own 'me'. It is better to limit the use of the word 'character' in rehearsal and look to the space instead. There the actor will find everything they need to bring the character to life. In old-fashioned theatre lore, there is a saying that you must only play the situation, and you must never play the character. That remains excellent advice. You can't find a character by excavating the character's soul. A character is a living, changing thing, created anew every second as it sees developing problems in the space around, and then attempts to solve them.

In short, Alex and Irina do themselves a favour by shifting the emphasis from getting *into* the character and onto only seeing what the character *sees*. As has already been said, they don't need to become the character (in fact, of course, they cannot), they just need to step into the character's space. They can give up fantasies of a fixed self behind Macbeth and Lady Macbeth, and let them be fluid and changeable and utterly dependent on the space around them.

⁓ Don't think about who your character is. Think about what your character sees.

There is an old theatre myth that Shakespeare is giving advice to actors through Hamlet's mouth when he gives notes to a company who are on tour to Elsinore. He encourages them to speak the speech *trippingly on the tongue*. This isn't always good advice. One-size-fits-all solutions rarely work anyway. Hamlet turns out to be as unreliable a theatre director as he is a revenge hero.

That said, Shakespeare has indeed hidden the mother of all advice to actors in *Hamlet*, and that is a question that can help every actor at every moment of every scene. It is the very first line of the play, when Bernardo asks, simply, '*Who's there?*' Never mind speaking the speech trippingly on the tongue. 'Who are you talking to?' is a question that quickly releases vast amounts of energy. 'Who are you talking to?' is so useful because it falls into a category of questions that are focused on what a character sees around them, not on who the character is.

To step into the character's shoes, ask what they see in the space. Questions about the internal experience of the character, their feelings, or their essential characteristics can mislead us into feeling superior. It's the character's reaction to what they see that will define who they are. And so the most useful questions are questions about the space. They are so simple they might seem stupid:

> Where are you?
> Who are you talking to?
> What do you see?
> Where is the problem?

At all costs avoid questions about character, like:

> How does Macbeth feel about this?
> Why did he choose to do that?

And never ask:

> How should we play this scene?

Even though they may seem reasonable and sensible, these 'how' and 'why' questions are treacherous. A character is not a computer programme that churns out the same solution to every problem. We can't possibly know what a character will do until they are tested by the space. At best, we can only imagine what they will probably do. 'How' and 'why' questions make us feel comfortable and in control, but these are false reassurances. They are the sort of questions that demand that Irina and Alex search inside themselves for answers. As soon as we search inside, we disconnect from the space. And above all, as soon as we start to ask them, let alone answer them, we may notice that our feet are hovering slightly off the ground. We are no longer looking at the characters horizontally through that tunnel. We are judging ever so slightly from on high. 'How' and 'why' questions are like riffling through a box of chocolates, as if you can pluck out an idea and impose it on the play.

⁂ Ask questions starting with 'what/where/who', not 'how/why'.

Let's put this key to work in a scene. Irina is working on Lady Macbeth's last scene in the play. She enters sleepwalking, while a doctor and a servant watch her. In this nightmare, she admits to her crimes. Until now, Macbeth and Lady Macbeth have been obsessed with dreaming. Sleep, night, blankets, darkness and nightmares are woven deep into the fabric of their text. Along with the dead baby, these are some of the most frequently recurring images in the play. We have already come across Lady Macbeth's obsession with sleep, when she drugged the guards:

> *'That death and nature do contend about them*
> *Whether they live or die.'*

She paints herself as some sort of Mistress of Sleep, a ruler over dreams and night-time: elsewhere she instructs her husband to be ruled by her in this *'great business'*,

> 'Which shall to all our nights and days to come
> Give solely sovereign sway and masterdom.'

But later her maid reveals that she must sleep with a light beside her because Lady Macbeth is so afraid of the dark. It is a fear that betrayed itself in her first scene, when the image of a little girl hiding and peeping under the covers leaked treacherously into her speech:

> 'Come, thick night,
> And pall thee in the dunnest smoke of hell,
> That my keen knife see not the wound it makes,
> Nor heaven peep through the blanket of the dark,
> To cry "Hold, hold!"'

It's a fear like her husband's. We have already heard Macbeth being tortured by a voice that tells him that *'Macbeth shall sleep no more, Macbeth has murdered sleep'*. For both, sleep is a terrifying place. Of course: because in our dreams we are completely alone. We sometimes use 'sleep together' as a euphemism for sex, a synonym for closeness. But sleeping together is the exact opposite. When we go to sleep next to someone we love, we say goodbye to them and go on a voyage each of us must make alone.

The Macbeths can't bear to be alone. They are clearly very close to each other at the start of the play, but the deed with which they intended to consummate their closeness in fact drives them apart for ever. They become self-conscious and embarrassed around each other, and no longer know how to be in a space together. Lady Macbeth keeps trying to fix this, paper over the cracks, and fan to life the dead ashes of their relationship. They may look away from the loneliness that looms over them, but when they go to sleep, they have to look that loneliness in the face.

Shakespeare sometimes uses dreams as a way of pulling back the veil and showing what it's like when we are not pretending that we are all right. Everything we have been suppressing during our waking hours comes to the surface, filtered through our dreams. He shows us just what happens when Lady Macbeth, the self-professed ruler of dreams, goes to sleep. Out of her dreams pour the terror, confusion, guilt and compassion that she's spent so long persuading us she doesn't have. It turns out that she can't after all '*stop up th'access and passage to remorse*' for a full five acts. When Lady Macbeth's suppressed humanity finally floods out, it will flow through the blood of her nightmares, until finally she kills herself.

At first glance, it would be easy to assume that this scene is a purely internal event. It's about Lady Macbeth's guilt, her dreamworld, and her conscience breaking out. Irina might think she needs to do a lot of portraying Lady Macbeth's character in order to get through this scene, but if she tries to do this, the scene runs the risk of becoming all about the how and why of her mental breakdown. But this, as we now know, is not the path to finding life. Let's try to look at the scene, not from the point of view of how we see (and judge) her, but more humbly to try to see what she sees.

LADY MACBETH
   Yet here's a spot.

DOCTOR
   Hark! she speaks. I will set down what comes from her, to satisfy my remembrance the more strongly.

LADY MACBETH
Out, damned spot! Out, I say! – One: two: why, then, 'tis time to do't. – Hell is murky. – Fie, my lord, fie! A soldier, and afeard? What need we fear who knows it, when none can call our power to account? – Yet who would have thought the old man to have had so much blood in him?

DOCTOR
Do you mark that?

LADY MACBETH
The Thane of Fife had a wife: where is she now? – What, will these hands ne'er be clean? – No more o' that, my lord, no more o' that: you mar all with this starting.

DOCTOR
Go to, go to. You have known what you should not.

GENTLEWOMAN
She has spoke what she should not, I am sure of that. Heaven knows what she has known.

LADY MACBETH
Here's the smell of the blood still. All the perfumes of Arabia will not sweeten this little hand. Oh, oh, oh!

DOCTOR
What a sigh is there! The heart is sorely charged.

GENTLEWOMAN
I would not have such a heart in my bosom, for the dignity of the whole body.

DOCTOR
Well, well, well.

GENTLEWOMAN
Pray God it be, sir.

DOCTOR
> *This disease is beyond my practice: yet I have known those which have walked in their sleep who have died holily in their beds.*

LADY MACBETH
> *Wash your hands, put on your nightgown; look not so pale. – I tell you yet again, Banquo's buried; he cannot come out on's grave.*

DOCTOR
> *Even so?*

LADY MACBETH
> *To bed, to bed! there's knocking at the gate: come, come, come, come, give me your hand. What's done cannot be undone. – To bed, to bed, to bed!*

Irina could start the rehearsal considering all the million possible ways of 'how' she could say the words:

> *'Yet here's a spot… Out, damned spot!'*

She could, for example, be making a joke out of the little spot; she could be struggling in frustration; she could be demanding help. We are told that the more choices we have, the freer we are. But this apparent abundance of choice is a useful red flag for the actor. Experience teaches us that as the stakes go up, our number of choices dwindle. Our friends will know that we have many more choices than we ourselves think we have. A friend might gently ask us if we really do need that fourth glass of whiskey. But from our own personal point of view there is only one good option.

So, if Irina spends her time wondering, 'How would Lady Macbeth say this line? Like this or… like that?' she's unconsciously elevating herself to a godlike position over the scene. Only Irina has many choices; Lady Macbeth feels she has none. That is because the stakes are far lower for Irina. The more Irina pays attention to Lady Macbeth's space, the more she will discover that it leaves Lady Macbeth very few options. The space is bigger than her, and it's telling her what to do.

To bring Lady Macbeth to life, Irina needs to see Lady Macbeth's space through Lady Macbeth's eyes, and her eyes alone, and perceive the specific set of problems that are forcing Lady Macbeth to speak. Irina needs to perceive her million choices start to boil down to one: the one solution to her space in that second. If she persists in feeling she has a plethora of choices about how to say the line, she has gone wrong.

Irina only has one kind of choice she can make: these are answers to concrete questions about what Lady Macbeth sees in the space: questions like 'What do I see?' and 'Who am I talking to?' and 'Where am I?' She needs to make detailed, specific answers to these questions. Having made her choices about the space, she must surrender to them. She will then discover that she has wonderfully few choices left about how to speak the line.

Here's a conundrum. It is only when the character feels trapped that the actor can start to feel truly free. The reverse is also true. If the character feels totally free in the space, then the actor will feel totally trapped. Nothing kills the imagination quicker than a blank canvas. And it is exhilarating for the audience to watch Lady Macbeth face what appears to her to be a choice-less situation, and to watch her struggle vainly for one last iota of control and freedom as she tries to solve an insoluble problem.

Here are the useful questions Irina might ask about her famous line, '*Out, damned spot!*' Her answers are, of course, up to her imagination, but she needs to make them as specific as possible. She can't start the scene with a general hunch: she needs to see the space first. She can't start speaking without first having something to react to. She cannot start by feeling. She needs to see vividly what Lady Macbeth is seeing. So Irina asks herself:

Who is she talking to?

The answer is up to the actor. It could be her mother, it could be herself projected out, it could be a friend. Irina decides that Lady Macbeth is speaking to a childhood friend. It's a friend she could run to when she was in trouble or afraid or lonely. She can see the exact expression on her friend's face.

Where is she?

Irina decides Lady Macbeth is back in the bathroom in the house where she grew up, standing at the basin. Her friend is watching approvingly as she gets rid of this stain on her hand.

What does she see when she sees the spot?

Irina decides that Lady Macbeth sees a sticky spot on her hand, which although small, smells awful. Irina decides that it is on the knuckle of the ring finger of her left hand.

Lady Macbeth's line is a reaction to this very specific space. This means Irina must see the space first before she can speak, even if this only takes a millisecond. Otherwise, she will be speaking into a void. Disaster. If she then starts to wonder how her character would feel – double disaster. The moment Irina finds herself wondering 'Now, how would Lady Macbeth say this line?' she knows that she is in trouble. How can she save the situation? She needs to make more and more concrete decisions about the space. As soon as she does, she will see that the space is engulfing her more and more completely, and more and more of Lady Macbeth's choices will vanish. She will reach a tipping point where she feels like there are no options left about how to speak the lines.

So Irina has found her first space, and her first impulse to speak. But Lady Macbeth is in a dream, and in the logic of dreams we jump-cut between locations. Halfway through a line, she suddenly crosses a threshold into a new space.

'One: two: why, then, 'tis time to do't.'

Irina asks her 'who/what/where' questions. Here's what she settles on this time:

Where is she?
She's gone back to the place where she was standing in the crucial moment when she rang the bell to signal to Macbeth that it was time to murder Duncan. We heard that very bell in the dagger speech we saw earlier. Lady Macbeth has jumped back to that watershed moment, the very last second in which she could have stopped the dreaded event.

What can she see?
She's got the bell in her hand. It's in the dark, in the middle of the night, and she must ring the bell in precisely the way that will alert Macbeth, but not wake the sleeping court. Not too quiet, not too loud.

Who can she see?
She decides she's speaking to the Macbeth in her mind's eye, whom she knows is somewhere else in the castle.

Answering these spatial questions gives plenty of potent instructions to her body and voice about what they must do. No sooner does she ring the bell than the dream hurls her over a new threshold into another space.

'Hell is murky.'

Again, Irina needs to explore the concrete reality of this new space: now she's in hell itself. She must see all this first *before* she is prompted to speak. She passes a threshold, and it is useful for her to remember that whatever she sees on the other side is surprising. Listen also to what she does not say about it. She doesn't say what we might expect of hell. It's not fiery, or hot, or filled with devils. She says something odd. It's *murky*. That's a strange word. So Lady Macbeth has found herself in hell, and it isn't at all what she thought it would be. Perhaps she was expecting hell to be full of red flames, like an altar painting in a church. Instead, what she is seeing is something different and discombobulating. Who could have foreseen that the Inferno has a power cut? Irina decides that she's calling through the foggy darkness to Macbeth, using the candle she's holding to try to see him through the dark.

We're only three lines into Lady Macbeth's text, and she's already been in at least three radically different spaces. The whole scene is composed of a series of miniature scenes. In the dream, the space metamorphoses rapidly. Every couple of lines, there is a new jump-cut, and Lady Macbeth crosses a new threshold. Each of these tiny scenes must be fully located in Irina's imagination. Irina's challenge is to notice when the space has changed, and then to be completely specific about who she is talking to and what she sees in each one. Each brief space must be clear and distinct. By the end of the scene, Irina reckons that Lady Macbeth has jumped between spaces fifteen times. She decides each of the following lines is in reaction to a different space:

'Yet here's a spot.'

'Out, damned spot! Out, I say!'

'One: two: why, then, 'tis time to do't.'

'Hell is murky.'

'Fie, my lord, fie! A soldier, and afeard? What need we fear who knows it, when none can call our power to account?'

'Yet who would have thought the old man to have had so much blood in him?'

'The Thane of Fife had a wife: where is she now?'

'What, will these hands ne'er be clean?'

'No more o' that, my lord, no more o' that: you mar all with this starting.'

'Here's the smell of the blood still. All the perfumes of Arabia will not sweeten this little hand.'

'Oh, oh, oh!'

'Wash your hands, put on your nightgown; look not so pale.'

'I tell you yet again, Banquo's buried; he cannot come out on's grave.'

'To bed, to bed! there's knocking at the gate: come, come, come, come, give me your hand. What's done cannot be undone.'

'To bed, to bed, to bed!'

Another actor might find a different number of spaces. That is all well and good, so long as they make sure that all these spaces are different and specific, and then let each materialise around them in a split second. They must look through Lady Macbeth's eyes as each new landscape wraps itself around her. They must look through Lady Macbeth's eyes as each landscape in the nightmare engulfs her, and only then react to it.

There is no denying that Irina faces an athletic task hurtling through these thresholds. But these 'who/what/where' questions give her a practical way of plugging into each different space and offer Irina something much more potent and concrete to work with than the vagueness of 'how' and 'why'. Asking how and why tends to lead the actor to a vantage point that is slightly superior, but also, like Lady Macbeth's hell, murky. Superiority is a deadly poison for any artist. Above all, the concrete 'who/what/where' questions will help Irina to see the space first. She will not discover life if she tries to build a character first. Everything that Lady Macbeth says and does, everything that Lady Macbeth is, is a reaction to the space. Even a line like

'Oh, oh, oh!'

might appear to be an expression of feeling. It is not. Even when we howl out in pain, we are reacting to the space where it is specifically located, and then doing something to fix it. Irina needs to put herself into the raw, unstable moment of the encounter, and not try to control it by asking 'how' and 'why'. Character cannot exist as a separate entity. It only exists in collision with the space.

So, Alex and Irina ask, is there anything we can rely on if we cannot rely on our characters? The answer is – you guessed it – the space. There is something lurking in the space that every character can depend on to release energy. And that is the subject of the next chapter.

PREDICAMENT

13

Imagine that a father is taking his young son fishing. It's raining, but the son insists on going anyway. As they drive, the rain comes down harder and harder, and soon the river is threatening to burst its banks. As the car stops, and before his father can stop him, the boy jumps out and tears down to the riverbank. The father sprints after him but before he catches up, the boy trips and falls headlong into the rushing water. The father manages to grab the little boy's ankle, and, with his other hand, seizes a gorse bush. His feet are slipping in the mud, the gorse is tearing his hand, and the boy's skin starts to turn blue.

Let's think about this moment. In the theatre we sometimes use the technical term 'given circumstances' to help us with a scene. This was an idea used a hundred years ago by Stanislavsky, and involves looking at how the environment affects the character. If Alex were playing the father in this scene, he might list the given circumstances as the cold, the wet, the mud, the speed of the river, the fact his son may drown, the mother waiting at home. All these facts inform the father's behaviour, the way he moves his body, and the choices he makes. Stanislavsky also talks about 'developing circumstances', or the way these external influences change through a scene. These undoubtedly remain a great creative tool. But Stanislavsky, in his wisdom, gave us another golden piece of advice. He said: '*Create your own method. Don't depend slavishly on mine. Make up something that will work for you! But keep breaking traditions, I beg you.*' So, at Stanislavsky's invitation, let's take a sideways look at the word 'circumstances'.

This word can sometimes be misleading. In English – and in Stanislavsky's Russian – it can imply a sense of neutrality. The word 'circumstance' comes from the Latin words for 'around' and 'to stand', even suggesting the image of passive bystanders. It can smuggle in a fudge. This fudge can contain a deadly poison: that the space may be neutral. The father, desperately clinging to his son's ankle, would never describe his experience as 'a set of circumstances'. His son is about to drown, and the man's grip on his ankle is slipping. The father's experience is not that he is in a set of circumstances. Instead, he's in a *predicament*. This word has proven much more useful in rehearsal. It acknowledges the precariousness of things. A predicament is the 'circumstances in jeopardy'. It reminds us to look for what is making the space dangerous.

You cannot remain neutral towards a predicament. We don't want to be rehearsing a play that takes place in a set of neutral circumstances. Certainly, no one would want to watch it. Indeed, any sense of neutrality will paralyse the actor, for if your character is manoeuvring in a neutral space, all your life energy will slowly drain away. You need to find a current for your character to swim against. Preferably a strong one. A predicament is a challenge in the space with which the character must do battle.

Now, a predicament isn't a general sense of danger in the space, something that is equal and the same for everyone. It is deeply personal and subjective to each character. When you look through any human being's green glasses, you will see a specific set of jeopardies that is making the space uniquely problematic for them. No two characters share exactly the same predicament, because they each see the space differently. Every passenger on the *Titanic* will have perceived the crisis slightly differently. But for each of them one thing must have been the same: their predicament was never a theoretical idea. It was always an actuality of the space. Predicament is a concrete problem that the character must combat. It shrinks the choices the character sees, and ensures the character can never feel fully in control. When the choices dwindle for the character, as Irina discovered in Lady

Macbeth's sleepwalking scene, the scene becomes more and more alive for the actor.

Let's go back to our scene by the river. Fortunately, the father holds on long enough for help to arrive. As the son sits under a shiny thermal blanket in the back of the ambulance, the local news team rolls in, rushes up to the father and says, 'You're a hero! What was it like? How did you manage to hold on for so long?' He may reply that anyone would have done the same. And he may be right. His predicament gave him no choice. He hung on simply because he felt there was nothing else he could do. In that awful moment he didn't have time to think about 'why'. Every scrap of his being, all sense of time and space, all feeling, all memory, was focused on his grip on the wet sock. The danger in the situation was so intense that he won't even be conscious of what he did. He just did it. It is almost as if the space decided for him. His predicament left him no choice.

Hamlet, Lady Macbeth and Othello all make extraordinarily bad decisions. Hamlet decides to obey the orders of a ghost; Lady Macbeth persuades her husband to kill the king when she could easily go back to the banquet and enjoy being the new Lady Cawdor; Othello murders his young wife on the flimsiest evidence. We sit in the audience, astonished that intelligent people can make such disastrous choices. However, we can only see this because of our privileged position of looking in from the outside, and from slightly above. It's the God problem again. We need to keep a check on where our feet are standing. The actor must always try to see the space horizontally from the character's point of view. Hamlet, Lady Macbeth and Othello each imagine they are trapped in their own personal nightmare, a corner where they have no choice. They each see a predicament that is so powerful that it threatens to overwhelm them.

Personally, it seems to me that the supreme moment in acting is when the actor turns to see the predicament. Circumstances, motive, situation – all evaporate in the heat of that encounter.

☞ Look for predicament.

Another useful description of a predicament might be: 'That which makes the story worth telling.' In fact, a predicament is the only thing that has ever made any story worth the telling. I loved the movie *Jaws*. I haven't seen it in several decades. But what do I remember? The moment when the giant shark whooshes out of the water with its huge blank eye, and someone exclaims: 'You're gonna need a bigger boat!' There's a predicament for you! I can still feel that in my guts. We often imagine that it's the characters or the plot that hook us into a play. But it's not. The thing that hooks us is the predicament. It's the thing which gives us a white-hot sense of personal connection to the play. A predicament is our hot-wire for empathy, and empathy beats at the heart of all good theatre.

Let's consider empathy for a moment. Empathy is not the same as sympathy. Sympathy is hard-wired into us; it's about imagining that another person is like us. We develop it by mirroring our mothers as a baby. The mother pulls a face, the baby pulls the same one back. She waves, the baby waves back. We learn by copying each other, in a ritual that soothes both adults and children alike. It is an essential first rung in our development. Sympathy is about building relationships through sameness.

Sympathy means 'I like you because you are like me.' This makes us feel secure. That's fine and dandy, until the day dawns when you discover you are not exactly like the other person. This discovery is inevitable. It's fine so long as you are a child, and you mirror your mother to say, 'I am like you, and you are like me.' But around the age of two, the child starts to feel that perhaps they don't like this game any more, and then the problem of different wills arises. And that goes on for the next eighty years or more.

If you believe you can only love someone who is just like you, the consequences are dire. Sympathy can build walls and start wars. Sympathy powers the idea that you are protecting your children and your family from other people who are not like you. Most people who go to war believe they are doing it out of sympathy, out of love. We must be very careful with managing our sympathy.

Empathy is completely different. It's much harder and less instinctive than sympathy. It is to do with understanding that I see you, but that you are standing in a different position from me. This can pose problems. Sympathy normally feels like a nice warm bath, that nice togetherness feeling, but all warm baths get cold. Empathy is about trying to see the world from another position, through another person's green glasses. My shoes are in a different position from your shoes. Empathy sustains love far better than sympathy, because empathy allows the other person to be different from you.

However, we can enjoy sympathy and be delighted when we come across people with whom we share things in common. But when it comes to our differences, we need to use our empathy, and that is more challenging. The theatre is not the place for sympathy. If we try to create moments in which everyone feels the same thing at the same time, it is a form of industrial writing. It might be very successful, but it is less like theatre and more like a mass rally.

We invite the audience to make the play with us by adding the active ingredient of their own imaginations. And we can't predict or control their imaginations or force them into seeing the same thing. If two people sitting next to each other have completely different ideas about what they are looking at, then that's fine. Normally that's brilliant – in the theatre. But as soon as we try to coerce the audience to feel sympathetic towards a character, we are inviting them to be sentimental. This leaves no room for ambivalence, no room for human uncertainty, no room for life. It's a one-dimensional relationship.

Empathy can achieve something much more profound. With empathy, good theatre can help us witness the intimate workings of another human being and go to places yet undiscovered in ourselves – often to places we are reluctant to go. Predicament is all about empathy, because it invites the audience not to think, 'I am just like this character!' but instead, 'I can imagine the position this character is in,' which is utterly different. It allows the audience to step into the character's shoes for themselves. If you can't find a predicament, there is no room for the audience's empathy.

What is a piece of theatre, really? It is a place where we can safely share our experiences of predicament. Everything in a piece of theatre – stories, characters, poetry and images – are delivery systems for a predicament. The struggle of the human versus the space is at the heart of all plays. It creates an electric current between the audience and the stage. It's impossible to imagine that you are somebody else. But we *can* imagine what we would feel if we faced the same problem, standing in the other person's shoes. Predicament is what allows the audience to get personal with the play and see themselves within it.

Think about Romeo and Juliet. It's hard to imagine what it's like to be teenaged medieval Italian aristocrats. However, we immediately connect with their predicament. The space is conspiring against them. Their nightmare is that they live in a space that is forcing them apart. That is what moves us, because we can imagine ourselves in that position. All of us dread Juliet's balcony, the thing that separates us from the person we love. We do not become involved with Romeo and Juliet because we identify with the characters, or even because the story is compelling. What hooks us into the play is their predicament.

There is a moment in *King Lear* when Regan and her husband Cornwall rip out Gloucester's eyes because they suspect he has been passing intelligence to the enemy. She says:

> '*Go thrust him out at gates, and let him smell*
> *His way to Dover.*'

The second half of this sentence is the brutal part. Shakespeare isn't great because he can write big complex thoughts. He is great because he knows what he doesn't need to say and what cannot be said. Good artists learn what to leave out. In just eight syllables, '*let him smell his way to Dover*', he ignites our empathy. He doesn't have to write 'Gloucester is blind'. That's a cold fact that we can 'understand'. Mere understanding doesn't do much to awake our empathy and implicate us bodily. Instead, Shakespeare rubs our noses in Gloucester's predicament. He forces us to imagine how Gloucester's blindness has made him utterly vulnerable to the space around him. He turns blindness from being a mere idea into a punch in the stomach, the epic physical struggle with the space. There is a carnal sensuality to the image, as we picture Gloucester's pink nostrils sniffing frantically at the air, trying to smell his way to safety. In a flash, we can imagine what it would be like to feel our own nostrils flaring, quivering against the wind, our remaining GPS in a suddenly dark world. A world that has vanished. A new world we were never prepared for. This is where we meet Gloucester as an equal human being, together in our smallness, facing, to put it mildly, a predicament.

There is no holiday outside of a predicament. You can't choose it or switch it on and off. It never happens that the actor is playing a scene in which there is no predicament. The circumstances always have danger in them. Even in the lightest of comedies, the character is facing some kind of disaster. It doesn't matter what the play is – it could be by Kane or Beckett, Pinter or Shakespeare, comedy or tragedy: looking for a predicament releases our imaginations.

At the beginning of *Much Ado About Nothing*, there's a spat between two old flames turned enemies, Beatrice and Benedick. Beatrice turns to Benedick and says:

> *'I wonder that you will still be talking, Signor Benedick: nobody marks you.'*

The stakes, at first glance, seem low. It's a funny line, and a great put-down. Say in rehearsal we decide that Beatrice will pour out some tea for her cousin Hero, as she says the line over her shoulder to Benedick. That seems to work well enough, and we can move on. But when we consider the possible predicament, this moment becomes much more powerful. There is more going on here than a barbed comment delivered on a whim. Through the play it slowly dawns on us that perhaps Beatrice is terrified of falling in love with Benedick. If she lets herself fall in love, Beatrice will no longer be Beatrice. Benedick's presence in the same space as her threatens to obliterate her. Now there's a very real predicament.

It is useful for the actor to think that somewhere, unconsciously, Beatrice feels that if she doesn't put him down, she may fall apart. What seems like a little put-down is intended to crush him at the centre of his being. It's a defence by attack. She feels she has no choice but to put him down. This is when acting potentially becomes a great, transgressive and revolutionary art. The actor playing Beatrice can say that line as if it's a whim, or they can say it as if it's a whim covering up a great pool of dread that she will be annihilated by Benedick. It can be the same staging, the same moment of time, delivering a put-down while pouring tea for Hero. Except this time there is a difference; this time it is infected with predicament.

If there is no pain, it's not funny. That's the essence of comedy. Comedy and tragedy are two sides of the same coin. Real humour is painful, because there is always a predicament at work. Later in *Much Ado*, Don Pedro says to Beatrice,

> 'You were born in a merry hour'

and she replies,

> 'No, sure, my lord, my mother cried; but then there was a star danced, and under that was I born.'

This is deeply moving because it is so full of pain. We may hear in it, 'My mother wishes I had never been born, but I'm okay, because I get to be the funny lady.' We realise that she's fed up with being the witty one. We all perform ourselves, but sometimes we just can't bear it any more. It can be exhausting and lonely.

Comedy without predicament offers us nothing apart from a passing giggle. Comedy full of predicament pierces us through the heart while we laugh.

Predicament isn't something an actor can perform, but it's crucial to bring the work to life. Thinking about predicament helps to open the actor to the space outside themselves. Irina and Alex cannot play the Macbeths' predicament. They can only play the scene. Instead, what they can do is to allow the Macbeths' predicament to feed their invisible work. They can consider predicament deeply as they picture the space, not as it is (for how can we know?), but as the Macbeths see it. They can allow this sense of predicament to infuse the space and infect their imaginations. Dreams often deliver predicament. They may have a complex and elaborate story, and on waking we forget the narrative details, but the sense of peace or unease may stay with us, all day long and maybe longer. But like every other aspect of the invisible work, in the performance itself, Irina and Alex must forget predicament and just play.

If the predicament is powerful enough, it will remember itself. For example, the actor playing Beatrice must never worry about trying to demonstrate the predicament in the scene. She doesn't have to indicate Beatrice's terror of falling in love with Benedick. In fact, she mustn't. All of this belongs in the invisible work. If she has paid proper attention to it when she's preparing, when she comes to play, she can empty her mind and trust that the invisible work will find its way in. It will saturate the scene with life.

Predicament is far more important than even dramatic action. Theatre totally depends on predicament. One of Shakespeare's greatest scenes has almost no dramatic action but is saturated with predicament. Towards the end of *Othello*, Desdemona is being helped to bed by her attendant Emilia. Any minute now we suspect that Desdemona's husband, Othello, will burst violently into the room. But the women never mention that. It's too big, too inescapable. So, they do everything else. They sing, Emilia makes jokes, talks about men and sex and money. All quite light. And in the audience, we feel sicker and sicker as we know they are avoiding the elephant in the room. And because we know, we feel implicated.

But what is Emilia's predicament? Well, she may see a terrified Desdemona who is pretending that all is well. And she perhaps imagines that the best thing for Desdemona is to keep her cheerful, stop her being worried, chatter away, put one foot in front of the other, and hope the problem will disappear. It sounds sickeningly familiar. There is no 'dramatic action' to speak of, but the scene is suffused with predicament, and the audience is riveted by this world of manic denial.

At the start of Beckett's *Happy Days* we meet Winnie. But she is buried up to her waist in a pile of sand. There's a predicament. But Winnie appears quite cheerful and begins the play with the rapturous line, '*Another heavenly day.*' But just how 'heavenly' can it be, we wonder, trapped like that? She seems entirely oblivious of her circumstances. As in many great plays, she fails to see the predicament she is in, while we in the audience see the predicament all too clearly. Sometimes the characters may indeed intuit that something is wrong and deny it by pretending that something else is the threat. Othello thinks his predicament is dealing with an unfaithful wife, but in the audience, we see his real predicament is quite different. His familiar creature, Iago, is controlling and isolating him and fingering his weaknesses. We can't put him right from the audience, though there are reports over the years of frustrated audience members shouting out: 'Can't you see he is lying, you fool?!'

Predicament is particularly useful in bringing three dimensions to even the smallest parts. Imagine we are back in rehearsals for *Macbeth*, and we're looking at the scene in which Macbeth instructs two murderers to kill Banquo. Oleg and Mitya are junior actors in the company, playing the two murderers. They are two of the smallest parts in the play, and they don't have much to say in this scene. Alex, as Macbeth, takes up almost all the airtime. Oleg and Mitya aren't expecting this to be a thrilling day's rehearsal. But when we feed in their predicament, things get much more interesting.

MACBETH

Was it not yesterday we spoke together?

FIRST MURDERER

It was, so please your highness.

MACBETH

Well then, now
Have you considered of my speeches? Know
That it was he in the times past which held you
So under fortune, which you thought had been
Our innocent self: this I made good to you
In our last conference, passed in probation with you,
How you were borne in hand, how crossed,
The instruments, who wrought with them,
And all things else that might
To half a soul and to a notion crazed
Say, 'Thus did Banquo.'

FIRST MURDERER

                    You made it known to us.

MACBETH

I did so, and went further, which is now
Our point of second meeting. Do you find
Your patience so predominant in your nature
That you can let this go? Are you so gospelled

To pray for this good man and for his issue,
Whose heavy hand hath bowed you to the grave
And beggared yours for ever?

FIRST MURDERER
                        We are men, my liege.

MACBETH
Ay, in the catalogue ye go for men;
As hounds and greyhounds, mongrels, spaniels, curs,
Shoughs, water-rugs and demi-wolves are clept
All by the name of dogs. The valued file
Distinguishes the swift, the slow, the subtle,
The housekeeper, the hunter, every one
According to the gift which bounteous nature
Hath in him closed; whereby he does receive
Particular addition from the bill
That writes them all alike: and so of men.
Now, if you have a station in the file
Not i' th' worst rank of manhood, say 't,
And I will put that business in your bosoms
Whose execution takes your enemy off,
Grapples you to the heart and love of us,
Who wear our health but sickly in his life,
Which in his death were perfect.

SECOND MURDERER
                        I am one, my liege,
Whom the vile blows and buffets of the world
Have so incensed that I am reckless what
I do to spite the world.

FIRST MURDERER
                      And I another
So weary with disasters, tugged with fortune,

That I would set my life on any chance,
To mend it, or be rid on't.

MACBETH
Both of you know Banquo was your enemy.

MURDERERS
True, my lord.

MACBETH
So is he mine; and in such bloody distance
That every minute of his being thrusts
Against my near'st of life: and though I could
With bare-faced power sweep him from my sight
And bid my will avouch it, yet I must not,
For certain friends that are both his and mine,
Whose loves I may not drop, but wail his fall
Who I myself struck down; and thence it is,
That I to your assistance do make love,
Masking the business from the common eye
For sundry weighty reasons.

SECOND MURDERER
                    We shall, my lord,
Perform what you command us.

FIRST MURDERER
                    Though our lives –

MACBETH
Your spirits shine through you. Within this hour at most,
I will advise you where to plant yourselves;
Acquaint you with the perfect spy o' th' time,
The moment on't; for't must be done tonight,
And something from the palace; always thought
That I require a clearness – and with him,
To leave no rubs nor botches in the work,

Fleance his son, that keeps him company,
Whose absence is no less material to me
Than is his father's, must embrace the fate
Of that dark hour. Resolve yourselves apart:
I'll come to you anon.

BOTH MURDERERS
We are resolved, my lord.

MACBETH
I'll call upon you straight: abide within.

The MURDERERS exit

Let's play the game again where we imagine how the scene ought to have gone.

> The murderers come in.
> Macbeth gives them the order to kill Banquo.
> The murderers leave.

But that doesn't happen. Instead, the murderers come in and Macbeth just talks and talks and talks. If Shakespeare wanted Macbeth to speak simply and directly, he would have done so. He was quite capable of putting a brutally brief command into Beatrice's mouth in *Much Ado About Nothing* with '*Kill Claudio!*' There appears to be very little dramatic action in the scene, other than this endless talking around the point. And Macbeth talks about the strangest things, including, at one point, a list of animals. What on earth is going on?

Let's put ourselves in the murderers' shoes and imagine what this space looks like to them. They have been summoned to the castle to see the king. That is overwhelming in itself. Further, they know he wants them to do something dodgy. They've been ushered in through a back door and into the heart of the seat of government. Before they even enter, they will already be feeling overwhelmed by the space. The expectation is that this should be a brisk business exchange in a quiet corner with an underling holding an envelope of used banknotes. But instead, they walk in to see the great man himself, and to deepen their confusion he spouts a pile of nonsense. He's uncomfortably chummy, giving them a bizarre amount of status. He is playing the wrong scene. He comes out with things like

'I to your assistance do make love.'

This is wildly inappropriate. He's the king, they are criminals-for-hire. The conversation isn't supposed to go like this. Let's listen to our common-sense alarm, which is ringing loudly because Macbeth is being so embarrassing. The murderers have no idea about how they should respond. They have never been in a situation remotely like this before. This is more than just uncomfortable for them: it's downright terrifying. From where they are standing, they see a powerful man with a reputation for military prowess behaving like a used-car salesman. To them, the stakes of saying the wrong thing soar. In short, the murderers don't know how to play the scene they've found themselves in.

⚬— The character often feels as if they have found themselves in the wrong space.

Let's step away from the murderers shivering through this horribly awkward moment and think about this key for a moment. Many of Shakespeare's characters come on stage and immediately tell us something along the lines of 'I don't fit in this space.' And this is not a problem exclusive to Shakespeare. Perhaps this feeling of not-belonging is central to the experience of being human. We go to all sorts of lengths to feel like we are part of a tribe. Shakespeare knew how to take this foundational predicament and escalate it so that space is a danger to the very existence of the vulnerable human on his stage.

For example, at the start of *Twelfth Night*, Viola gets shipwrecked on the shores of Illyria. Her first words are:

> '*What country, friends, is this?*'

She's in a strange land, full of the absence of her drowned brother, with no way of surviving on her own. She doesn't know how to exist in this space, in the face of this predicament. Her reaction is extreme. She becomes someone else entirely. She becomes Cesario.

Or take Hamlet's very first line:

> '*A little more than kin and less than kind.*'

It's a weak pun in response to the new king Claudius, who has just called him his 'son'. It's a smart-alec reply about how Claudius is more family than he ought to be, as both his uncle and his stepfather. It's supposed to be funny, but this excruciating attempt to sound clever and in control reveals Hamlet's deep discomfort in the space he finds himself in. He's at court and he must face the fact that his mother condoned the choice of his uncle as the new king, by marriage, overlooking Hamlet. It's a very public moment after Claudius's coronation, in which Hamlet is under pressure to play ball and pretend it's all okay that he has been shoved into the shadows by his own mother. It's extraordinarily humiliating. He finds himself in the wrong space. He is most at home in a library at the University of Wittenberg. The court is not his comfort zone. In short, Hamlet is a fish out of water. His predicament is overwhelming. Hamlet does not know how to be Hamlet here. All of this leaks out in his weak pun.

And that's similar to what's going on with the murderers. They don't know how to play the scene they have found themselves in. They also feel like fish out of water. Macbeth drowns them in words, and their cautious responses reveal just how embarrassed they feel. What on earth are they supposed to say? Take, for example, the bewildering questions that Macbeth lands on them:

> 'Do you find
> Your patience so predominant in your nature
> That you can let this go? Are you so gospelled
> To pray for this good man and for his issue,
> Whose heavy hand hath bowed you to the grave
> And beggared yours for ever?'

What is he talking about?! The murderer answers:

> 'We are men, my liege.'

In his brevity, you can hear him angling for a safe position. It's a non-answer; strictly true, but least likely to put him in hot water. The poor murderer! He didn't walk in here expecting a philosophical interrogation about human nature, religion and his personal sense of justice. He came in expecting brief instructions and a quick payment. Even worse, in this barrage of words, Macbeth fails to give them the basic information they need, about when, where and how he wants Banquo killed. As a result, they are not sure exactly what they are being asked to do. If they had more status, they could stop him mid-flow and say, 'Sorry, what is it you actually want?' Instead, they must stand there, sweating, and wondering if they are going to get out of this room in one piece.

Their predicament is, as always, about the jeopardy that destabilises the space. They walked into the castle and found that it was exponentially more unpredictable and dangerous than they had expected. They don't know where to stand, what to say, or how to give Macbeth what he wants. Now, of course, they can't act the 'state' of being out of their depth. What they can do is spend every second scanning for signs and signals amid the chaos, and working out how on earth they should respond. Each second is a miniature move in a terrifying game of chess.

Hopefully, by considering the murderers' predicament, Oleg and Mitya have transformed a potentially boring rehearsal into something alive. Now the scene they create together will have infinitely more depth and life. Predicament will always help you. Even the spear-carrier with no lines in an obscure history play has a predicament. Find it, because the audience's empathy – and the character's life – depend on it.

DREAD

14

Some actors are liberated by the question, 'What does your character want?' Good. But others can feel constricted. The question seems to be very reasonable, but even very talented actors can become unstuck when asked it, particularly if it becomes insistent. Why? Well, often we ourselves don't know what we want, and therefore to answer the question for a character can be frustrating. We can usually only grasp the 'whys' and 'hows' of our own odd behaviour with the luxury of hindsight. It's a comforting fantasy to imagine that the character always knows what they want and will act accordingly. Knowing what we want is often not our experience of the present moment and this can become even more extreme as the stakes go up.

Let's come back to Macbeth and ask him why he kills Duncan. He might say, 'Well, it's obvious: because I want to become King of Scotland.' This seems perfectly logical. The problem is that it is only convincing for a while. It doesn't really wash. We never really know *why* he does it. *He* never really knows why he does it. As soon as he's king we never see him enjoying it. Even before he becomes king, he never fantasises about how good it would be to be king. Most of the time, he doesn't seem to want to do it at all. In fact, he spends much of his time telling us why he *shouldn't* kill Duncan. His reasons are deeply unclear and deeply human. If Alex thinks *Macbeth* is just a thriller about an ambitious man who wants to become King of Scotland, he will start to find the play boring. And so will we.

The problem is that being a human involves mystery. We often can't explain ourselves. Sometimes what we do surprises us. You may ask yourself questions like 'Why did I explode like that?', 'Why am I eating a second doughnut?', 'Why have I let myself run late for this important meeting?' This is frightening. We love the idea of rational reasons because they are very reassuring in the face of a chaotic universe. We are reassured that there's an explanation for suffering, horror and appalling violence. But we have to grow up and learn to tolerate mystery. When I am directing a play, my job is to make everything as clear as I can, while expecting that if the play is any good, it will have central mysteries that elude me. Mystery isn't something particularly esoteric, it's just part of our everyday experience. We can look at Macbeth and ask, 'Why would somebody do something they don't really want to do when they must know it will destroy them? Why would somebody destroy themselves?' Well, take a good look around – and welcome to life!

Of course we must try to understand ourselves, but it's prudent to accept that we never fully will. We should ask why the woman stabbed her roommate ninety-one times, and why the Macbeths tear themselves apart. Those are the kind of human questions we have a duty to examine. But we also must accept that ultimate defeat is probably inevitable. If we find ourselves saying 'I have completely understood it!', we can be sure we've completely missed the point. Understanding is sometimes nothing more than a form of control.

We might ask, 'Why ask a question that can't be answered?' And the reply must be: 'Because those are perhaps the best questions we can ask.' This is what it feels like to make plays. We go into the theatre – we act, we design, we direct – because we love our job. We feel compelled to. We do not love it for a cold, hard, factual reason. Human experience is not about knowing what we want and trying to achieve it. It would be easier if life were like that, but it isn't. Neither are good plays.

So, what would be a better question than 'What does the character want?' Perhaps ask the opposite. Don't just look for the pull: look for the push. Stop looking for the carrot, and pay attention to the stick. If you ask me what I want, it could make me panic. I often have no idea! On the other hand, it's far easier to see what I *don't* want. I could go on for hours with some very specific answers: 'I don't want to get Covid… I don't want to feel cold… I don't want to…' You can always rely on what you don't want. Why? Perhaps because there is always a predicament. We can always find a threat in the space around us. And often that threat has a dark shadow that makes it even more disturbing. A good name for that shadow is 'dread'.

⊕— **Don't search for what the character wants. Look for what they dread.**

Human beings have never been strangers to dread. It is a hugely important engine. Our mothers dreaded us dying, and so we have survived. Young parents are overwhelmed by the joy of a newborn child, but the joy is instantly counterbalanced by the dread of the baby dying. Dread is self-sufficient. You do not have to generate it. It's just part of the fabric of being human. It is behind some of our great achievements as a species. When you look at the big monuments, like Stonehenge, or Newgrange in Ireland, you realise that they are all built on dread: a fear that the sun might not come up next year, that the harvest will fail, that the god will get angry. It's not so far from an advert for a luxury watch. There's a dad and his young son boarding a yacht. The slogan is, 'You never own a [*insert brand here*] watch, you just look after it for the next generation.' It's trying to control time and make death bearable. It is about cancelling dread.

But dread will always be there, bubbling away, from the lowest-stakes situations to the highest. If you are looking for a flat, say, and you find the perfect one, you think, 'That's a great flat!' But immediately, in a nanosecond, you think, 'Oh my God, I'll lose it, someone else will get it.' Dread is never more than one click away. Imagine you are waiting for a friend in a café. We tend to feel uncomfortable and give ourselves something to do, like checking our phone or ordering another coffee. Why do we do this? There is nothing new on our phone. Is it because we have the slight sense of dread of having absolutely nothing to do? If our brains are empty, are we somehow vulnerable? We are always aware, somewhere, however slightly, of our vulnerability in the space, and always trying to make ourselves feel slightly safer.

It is useful to assume that dread is hard-wired into us. It's always whirring away in our brains, defending us from any potential danger. The problem is that dread isn't always specific. We can feel a sense of dreadful unease without having something to attach it to. Often, dread has a fuzzy outline, and this is frightening. Roosevelt came near to it when he said, 'We have nothing to fear but fear itself.'

So we invent causes. Think of a little girl pretending to be a ghost. She may throw a sheet over herself and run around the house shouting, 'Whoooo! Whooooo!' Why is a white sheet such a universal cliché for a ghost? It's because we imagine that ghosts are invisible, and in order to make them visible, they need to put clothes on. They need to 'vest'. We throw a white sheet over them to demonstrate where the invisible thing is. We have an underlying dread of the shapeless, which wants to dress itself in something explicable. If we can locate it in a concrete thing in the space, then we feel much better about it. We make this amorphous pool of dread vest itself in something specific, to help give it an outline. It's another way of putting ourselves back in control.

Perhaps one of Nietzsche's most intriguing observations was that human beings invented guilt in order to explain the randomness of suffering. We can't tolerate the fact that a plague or a crop failure could be a random event, so we invented reasons to make us feel in control of this randomness. We started saying things like 'I have caught the plague because I did something bad.' I may be bad but at least I am not powerless. We cannot bear our own bottomless dread. We will do anything to hang it on something. Every atom of our being fights against powerlessness.

But even when dread puts on clothes, it won't always wear them for very long. It will slip out of them and into another costume. A hypochondriac will find a lump on one foot one day and then, when the biopsy comes back negative, they will discover a new symptom somewhere else. In the same way, no one can ever get rid of dread. If we deal with it in one guise, it will rear its head in another.

Actors can waste a lot of time searching for what a character wants. It is much more useful to look for the dread. They will flounder if they anxiously search for a positive feeling that will compel their character to do things. Rehearsal experience has taught me that they will get further and faster if they search for the negative feeling to react against. It gives them much more energy than trying to turn themselves into little factories of positive volition. When Romeo is under the balcony, and the actor thinks his task is to radiate joy in his love for Juliet, the scene will get boring very quickly. But if, say, he is terrified to lose her, or fears that she may find him stupid and ordinary, then the actor will get somewhere. He has something to work against.

It is therefore much more useful for Alex and Irina to think that most of their energy comes not from what the Macbeths desire, but from what they dread. As we have seen, it's unclear why Macbeth kills Duncan, apart from the strange fact that he himself seems really frightened that he won't. What terrifies him most is that he is going to fail. It's similar with Lady Macbeth. She spends most of her time talking about how she fears that Macbeth won't be 'man' enough to kill Duncan. But, remarkably, she never tells us how much she wants to be queen. They almost seem to think they will have achieved their purpose if they can conquer their fear. It is not their will but their dread of failure that seems to drive them blindly forwards.

Alex and Irina may find it useful to think that both Macbeths dread being alone. At the beginning of the play, it appears, they have lost a child, an event that often drives the strongest of couples apart. They are lonely, and desperate to hang on to each other. Their fantasy, perhaps, is that the death of Duncan will somehow unite them finally in a great orgasmic act, and they won't feel alone any more. But of course, reality has exactly the opposite effect. Indeed, from the moment they commit the murder they are entirely isolated from each other.

Dread lies behind even the most apparently frivolous plays. Think of *The Importance of Being Earnest*, which its author Oscar Wilde called 'a trivial comedy for serious people'. So where is the dread? One way of looking at the characters in the play is that they are absolutely terrified of being ordinary, all speaking in such a self-regarding way. Gwendolen says of her diary, '*One should always have something sensational to read on the train.*' Miss Prism has the line, '*The chapter on the fall of the Rupee you may omit. It is somewhat too sensational for a young girl.*' Our common-sense alarm bell should go off at this strange, inflated way they all speak. What's behind this? What unites these characters is possibly their dread of seeing how ordinary they are. They are absolutely terrified to discover that their faeces smell the same as anybody else's.

This same dread of ordinariness is embedded in Chekhov's *Three Sisters*. Irina, the youngest sister, is upset that she can't remember the Italian word for 'window'. They are surviving by feeling superior to their uneducated neighbours. They look down on the townspeople, and only socialise with the officers from the local regiment. They dread being engulfed by the town, in case it turns out that they too are… well, ordinary. They spend so much of the play saying that they wish that they could go to Moscow, and Chekhov goes out of his way to point out how easy it would be for them to hop on the train and get there. So why don't they just leave? Dread. If they went to Moscow, they wouldn't be special there. It's an astounding play about stasis. They are stuck. They can't go forwards or back, because both directions are terrifying. Behind the apparent stillness we can see intense striving, fuelled by dread.

Dread is always a good tool to enable us to walk in another person's shoes. There is going to be dread somewhere, if you look hard enough. There is always a predicament to be dreaded. And usually that dread is just one or two taps away on the keyboard of our brains. It is already there, 'good to go'. You can try to play someone who is relaxed, but it's a losing game. Nobody, ever, is totally relaxed, and certainly never in a play. Some people may appear to be completely at ease, but it is a performance. There is always energy involved in just keeping it together in the face of our dread. To appear calm on the surface, we are repressing something underneath.

Of course, I'm not saying that people walk around the streets consciously terrified that they might fly apart. But dread is there, somewhere, underneath everything. We often discover *in extremis* that this unpleasant sensation of being about to disintegrate with dread is already one beat away. All of us feel like we are in the centre of our own epic stories. Just keeping it together can feel like a mighty task. Sometimes we look at a person sitting opposite us on the bus, and we might make an immediate judgement about them: that they are quite ordinary. But maybe, just maybe, that person is a hero fighting to keep themselves together. Perhaps they feel they are at the centre of an epic battle to survive.

If you supply this as a key to a character, it is amazing what riches it may yield. There is an already unconscious threat to the Prozorovs in *Three Sisters*, to Lady Bracknell in *The Importance of Being Earnest*, or to Benedick and Beatrice in *Much Ado About Nothing* – the indignation of these characters implies that they feel that with one false move they will fall apart. They are powered by dread. They are always having to face some enormous threat to their sense of existence.

Back to rehearsal. The Macbeths have been crowned king and queen. They are about to throw a banquet to celebrate their coronation, but Macbeth has terrified himself yet again. He has ordered two strangers to murder his closest friend, Banquo, and he cannot cope.

LADY MACBETH
Nought's had, all's spent,
Where our desire is got without content:
'Tis safer to be that which we destroy
Than by destruction dwell in doubtful joy.

Enter MACBETH

How now, my lord! Why do you keep alone,
Of sorriest fancies your companions making,

Using those thoughts which should indeed have died
With them they think on? Things without all remedy
Should be without regard: what's done is done.

MACBETH
We have scorched the snake, not killed it:
She'll close, and be herself, whilst our poor malice
Remains in danger of her former tooth.
But let the frame of things disjoint, both the worlds suffer,
Ere we will eat our meal in fear, and sleep
In the affliction of these terrible dreams
That shake us nightly. Better be with the dead,
Whom we, to gain our peace, have sent to peace,
Than on the torture of the mind to lie
In restless ecstasy. Duncan is in his grave;
After life's fitful fever he sleeps well;
Treason has done his worst: nor steel, nor poison,
Malice domestic, foreign levy, nothing,
Can touch him further.

LADY MACBETH
Come on.
Gentle my lord, sleek o'er your rugged looks;
Be bright and jovial among your guests tonight.

MACBETH
So shall I, love; and so, I pray, be you.
Let your remembrance apply to Banquo;
Present him eminence, both with eye and tongue:
Unsafe the while, that we must lave our honours
In these flattering streams, and make our faces
Vizards to our hearts, disguising what they are.

LADY MACBETH
You must leave this.

MACBETH

O, full of scorpions is my mind, dear wife!
Thou know'st that Banquo, and his Fleance, lives.

LADY MACBETH

But in them nature's copy's not eterne.

MACBETH

There's comfort yet; they are assailable;
Then be thou jocund: ere the bat hath flown
His cloistered flight, ere to black Hecate's summons
The shard-borne beetle with his drowsy hums
Hath rung night's yawning peal, there shall be done
A deed of dreadful note.

LADY MACBETH

What's to be done?

MACBETH

Be innocent of the knowledge, dearest chuck,
Till thou applaud the deed. Come, seeling night,
Scarf up the tender eye of pitiful day,
And with thy bloody and invisible hand
Cancel and tear to pieces that great bond
Which keeps me pale! Light thickens,
And the crow makes wing to the rooky wood.
Good things of day begin to droop and drowse,
While night's black agents to their preys do rouse.
Thou marvell'st at my words: but hold thee still;
Things bad begun make strong themselves by ill.
So, prithee, go with me.

Well, where is the dread in this scene? Lady Macbeth starts by telling us clearly that she is full of dread. She describes herself as '*without content*'. She thought that killing Duncan would transform her into the villainous diva she needed to be. So feeling '*the future in the instant*' didn't quite work out. She even says:

> '*Tis safer to be that which we destroy*
> *Than by destruction dwell in doubtful joy.*'

But then Macbeth walks in, and she changes her tune immediately. She rebukes him for seeming to wallow in self-pity and tells him in effect to just move on. She has a kind of insane, optimistic logic. The murder is over and done with, so there is no point in having feelings about it.

> '*Things without all remedy*
> *Should be without regard: what's done is done.*'

It isn't so simple. There are always consequences. It's absurd, because we know that Lady Macbeth feels the same as Macbeth does. She just told us so! So what is she up to? She seems to be fighting her own dread by turning her husband into a project she can fix. We should be very cautious of making someone our project, because often it is ourselves we would like to change. We see her buttoning herself up as soon as Macbeth comes in, denying the feelings she has just told us she has. Almost all her lines to him are instructions to keep it together. But they are just as much instructions for herself. Irina can think of this scene as a struggle to put a straitjacket on her husband's dread – and on her own.

Let's look at the scene from Macbeth's point of view. Lady Macbeth's question to him is:

> '*Why do you keep alone?*'

But the really interesting question is (as always) what has made him come into the space. He's not keeping alone. He's come to seek her out. And it is dread that is driving him through that door. He dreads being on his own, because he's just set in motion something unspeakable. He's ordered the murder of his best friend, and it seems he can't bear to be with himself. So perhaps he needs her physical presence to keep him together, his so-called *'partner of greatness'*.

But as soon as he enters, other dreads flood in. One of them is that they may turn on each other and compound their loneliness. He already feels adrift from her and everything else. If he tells her out loud what he has done, she might reject him completely. Somewhere he must disgust himself. He needs her love, but all she does, when faced with his torment, is to tell him to pull himself together.

'You must leave this.'

He replies with an agonising scream:

'O, full of scorpions is my mind, dear wife!'

It's the closest they ever get to connecting. He reaches across the space to his beloved wife and tries to share his pain with her. It's the nearest they ever get to admitting their dread in each other's presence. He then very nearly tells her what he has done, minutes earlier, in condemning Banquo to death.

'Thou know'st that Banquo, and his Fleance, lives.'

But even then, the admission is too terrible to say out loud. He dreads putting words to it. If we say things out loud, they might actually exist. As always in this play, Macbeth can't face what he has done. Just like his wife, Macbeth is trying not to disintegrate in the face of dread. But it bursts out and it scares him. He has admitted his terror. *'Dear wife'* is shockingly tender. This sudden intimacy of admitting his dread makes him vulnerable. It makes him admit he is not in control. And in response to this, Lady Macbeth replies:

'But in them nature's copy's not eterne.'

He's like a drowning man, but has she has just thrown him a lifeline? She seems to have implied – very obliquely – that Banquo and Fleance will die. He hears her take away some of his responsibility and share the burden. Immediately his tone changes. He finds the energy to haul himself back together behind the mask of a guy who is in control. He replaces the vulnerability with the performance of a clever mastermind.

> *'There's comfort yet; they are assailable;*
> *Then be thou jocund: ere the bat hath flown*
> *His cloistered flight, ere to black Hecate's summons*
> *The shard-borne beetle with his drowsy hums*
> *Hath rung night's yawning peal, there shall be done*
> *A deed of dreadful note.'*

We should listen to the difference between '*dear wife*' and '*dearest chuck*' a few lines later. The first is achingly vulnerable, the second sounds jaunty and cocksure. Between the two, he's managed to put a gigantic lid on his volcanic feelings and plaster on horror clichés to pretend he is in control. He is talking about Hecate again – more bullshit.

Just keeping it together has become a daily struggle for them both. Macbeth warns Lady Macbeth that they need to

> *'Make our faces vizards to our hearts.'*

But strapping on the mask of normality is an increasing challenge. So much of their energy is going into simply holding themselves together: an exhausting task for the characters, but one that is a massive source of free energy for Alex and Irina.

Macbeth kills Duncan to exterminate his dread. Duncan's presence in the castle was a pulsating engine of dread, and it filled every corner of Macbeth's imagination. But no sooner is Duncan dead, than that dread morphs into another form. It puts on clothes as Banquo, the man who the weird sisters prophesy will father a whole '*line of kings*', and later in the play he gasps in horror as Banquo's descendants march in procession past him.

Macbeth looks at Banquo and sees a real hero, a man who is kingly in his very nature. '*And in his royalty of nature reigns that which would be feared.*' He fantasises that Banquo is a better man than Macbeth will ever be. His very presence at court is a daily reminder to Macbeth that he is a grubby, treacherous, cowardly murderer. Most tellingly, he says, '*There is none but he whose being I do fear.*' Banquo's '*being*', note: not his '*doing*'. It's his very existence that threatens Macbeth. He's attached his sense of dread to Banquo's living, breathing existence. His dread has vested in the body of his best friend.

This is how the Macbeths career through the play, lurching from one dread, only to find the white sheet covering something else. They are like two children who have dared each other to go into a forest at night. They screw up their courage, hold each other by the hand, and creep into the wood. Inside it gets darker and darker, the night gets thicker and thicker. First, the trees start to lose their outline, and then the trees seem to get bigger and bigger. But in their fear, these two child Macbeths lose each other's hands. They get anxious and call out to each other, but their little voices get fainter and fainter. Now they can't make out any shapes at all in this undifferentiated night, and so they stray deeper and deeper into the darkness and lose each other completely. They are driven through the play by their dreads, and by goading each other to face up to them. But dread, like the trees, is bigger than they are.

Dread can become so overwhelming that death can seem a better option. We know this, because people kill themselves. Whatever dread they are facing must seem worse than death. All tragic characters are going through slow suicides as they run away from their dread. Hamlet, Macbeth and Othello give themselves disastrous tasks that are so obviously going to end badly. Hamlet gives himself the task of killing Claudius. Othello gives himself the task of proving Desdemona's infidelity. Macbeth gives himself the task of killing an old man who loves him.

We sit in the audience and watch them career towards destruction. But never mind what are they running towards: what exactly are they running *from*? Dread. But dread is formless, and so they need to give it a shape. Each character will fix their dread in a different way, and as one fix fails, dread will vest somewhere else. It's useful to imagine that every character has some nameless dread that pre-dates the play, and that during the action they will clothe it in different disguises. This gives the character the huge reassurance that they are in control of, and not the victim of, their predicament.

People may well desire and want things. For the actor, however, it is much more useful to translate desire into dread of loss. Trying to act positive desire can block the actor. Instead of looking at what we want, we should try looking at the exact opposite. But the expression 'what I don't want' can smuggle in unhelpful passivity. What we dread will release much more energy.

15
FALSE WORDS

Words are treacherous. They do not deliver what they claim on the tin. They appear to be labels that tell us what things mean. But meaning itself is a questionable idea. An actor can study carefully what the words mean, pour meaning into their performance, and the scene can still be dead. If we try to reduce everything to meaning, we normally end up just swapping facts. Most human communication has nothing to do with swapping facts. Words only work, more or less, when we are talking about basic information. 'It's raining', 'The house is on fire': fine. But if we want to do anything more than that, words are a very limited tool.

We use them to try to communicate experience, but human experience is often ambiguous and illogical. Certainly, with important experiences, the mere meaning of a word starts to feel inadequate. It barely scratches the surface. You can't ask someone what a rose means, or for that matter what their child means, because these things are not of that order. A child does not need meaning to live. A child does not need meaning to be loved. Words only admit to logic. Each word is a Trojan horse for logic. They smuggle in the delusion that it is possible to describe the indescribable. We sometimes imagine that if we can name something, we can understand it, and if we can understand it, we can control it.

So, in a way, all words can be treacherous. They have an agenda. They naturally resist a world that's mysterious or inexplicable. Art helps save us from the potential tyranny of logic. In short, we need art to rescue us from words. Take Constance's line, who fears for her son, Arthur, in Shakespeare's play *King John*: '*Grief fills the room up of my absent child.*' If you try to paraphrase these words, they become flat. The line is extraordinary because it seeks to share all sorts of things with us, not so much in the words but around the words; in fact, *despite* the words. Shadows shift and flit around the line, ghosts haunt the edges of the text. Does '*room*' not sound like 'womb' here? And how can something '*absent*' fill something else up? So it is grief that is doing the filling, as if it's a monster living in the room with her… These hints of images put us in touch with something that's enormous and unspeakable. Although we can never encapsulate what Constance is trying to share, we still empathise with Constance. Where the words fail, human life floods in. Words are dangerous when we think they can sum up our feelings literally, but are more helpful when we acknowledge they work in enigma.

Another challenge for the actor is that what the words are supposed to *mean* and what they are *doing* are often two things at war with one another. So what are words doing? All words, like everything else we do, are attempts to control the space. All attempts to control the space are ultimately futile. This is true of even the simplest text. If I were to say to you, 'It's a lovely day,' it's not really about the day. I'm saying it because I'd like you to think that I'm happy, or well intentioned, or optimistic, or maybe I want to cheer you up. I'm trying to change you. The words aren't a neutral description of the day. They are gestures of control, however well intentioned.

Trying to control someone doesn't have to be sinister. A mother rocking her baby and telling them they are safe is making a loving gesture of control. Now, the big problem (in fact, possibly the biggest problem ever) is that this, of course, isn't true. It isn't true because, for example, an asteroid could land on them and instantly destroy them. But few of us would thank their mothers for saying, 'I'm holding you now, darling, but we're not really safe because at any moment – an asteroid could fry us to a crisp.' We need a beautiful lie to begin our lives. But then we also need to be weaned off it. The important thing is that words aren't just the descriptions they pretend to be. They are weapons in our struggle to control the space. Every word we utter is intended to change the world.

Just like all other attempts to control the space, words are ultimately futile. They try to apply meaning to things that are beyond meaning. As a result, they never completely work. Every line of text in every play is a failure. It's an attempt to communicate an experience that words cannot deliver. Using words is like trying to make an oil painting using children's crayons. When Shakespearean characters have long speeches, it is not because they are perfectly encapsulating a human experience. It is because every line has failed, so they must try again. Indeed, the longer a character speaks, the more they are failing to communicate. Hamlet doesn't churn out soliloquy after soliloquy because he's good at describing his internal turmoil. It's because he can't find the right words. If he could, it would be a much shorter play. Words are there to help us to convey experience, but experience cannot be conveyed just by words. So words are always failing us. Words are fine, but we need to realise that they have serious limitations.

⚘ Words fail.

Shakespeare is not a genius because his words perfectly capture what it is to be human. Shakespeare is a genius because he understands that words are deeply limited. He knew that words are perhaps most alive when we grasp their failure. For example, the finest expression of love that I know is not from the iconic *Romeo and Juliet*, but a few words in an essay written just a few years earlier by Michel de

Montaigne. The love of his life, Étienne de la Boétie, had died when they were both young, and Montaigne had never recovered from the loss. Decades later he was able to write:

'If you force me to explain why I loved him, all I can say is, "It was because it was him, because it was me."'

That is all. Because it was him, because it was me. No more to say, because no more can be said. The words touch us because they articulate a tremendous silence, pregnant with the possibility of humanity. We know what that feels like. They are an attempt to say, 'I can't describe it.' Shakespeare, we know, did read Montaigne. But he did not need to. He knew the same thing as the Frenchman: at every moment that is most vividly human, there are no satisfactory words. We hear at a funeral, 'I've got no words…' And, of course, we haven't.

King Lear shelters from the storm in a broken-down hovel, his grandiose trappings shorn away. Destitute, humiliated and stripped of pomp, he finds himself next to a naked tramp: Edgar in disguise. He encounters this wretch freezing his arse off, standing uncomfortably close, within smelling distance. What words will he use? Amongst other epithets, Lear cries out, '*Thou art… the thing… itself!*' He is overwhelmed by the immediate bodily presence of a suffering human being. Experience will just not fit itself neatly into words. Lear must sit with this immediate human suffering. He shares the same human flesh.

Lear experiences the utter collapse of language. Words have let him down. Words are dead things. There's no such thing as a living word. Words are dead tools that we use to try to connect us to a living experience. We do not use words to describe our internal experience. We wrestle with words as we try to control the space.

There are many things that we can never explain. Of course, sometimes we do try, and sometimes afterwards we may feel we have betrayed something deeply precious. Because what was intended as truth has come out like a lie. All too often, we hear heartfelt words come out of our mouths, and afterwards want to cry, with T. S. Eliot's Prufrock, '*That is not what I meant at all. That is not it, at all.*' We may feel stupid because we cannot properly express ourselves. But, then again, nor can the cleverest person in the whole world. In fact, if I ever flatter myself that I'm perfectly formulating a thought with these words, it's a red flag that I'm probably talking perfect nonsense. The real effort to communicate is sweaty and imperfect. Anything truly human will distort when viewed through the prism of words. And, further, it's very often the things for which we have no words that are the most important things. The most important things happen when words fail. As a result, the actor's task goes far, far beyond simply delivering the meaning of the words.

We live in an increasingly wordy world. We're addicted to words. And in a way, words go out of their way to increase our addiction. There is a lie embedded in our culture that 'in the beginning was the word'. It is not so much our foundational myth as our foundational lie. For in the beginning was not the word. Before the word there was impulse, then there was breath, then there was movement, sound, music, dance – all sorts of things – before words came along. And in fact, we make words by vibrating our vocal cords with movement. No, words don't come first.

We communicate with each other instinctively, using our whole body. Words are only a very small part of the experience. With good actors, almost everything is expressed by the body. Words often get in the way of our sharing the thing we are talking about. Yes, they can be efficient, but we should remember that every new efficiency means a loss. Words take something messy and carnal and turn it into a cool theory. They can make the grubby thought seem tidy. And they can cause us to effectively 'dis-experience' things.

We tend to package things in certain words to make them more palatable to ourselves and others. They may help us dis-experience an uncomfortable reality. For example, one could argue that 'manifest destiny' really means 'murder our way to the Pacific'. Words can act like an anaesthetic, numbing us to a painful reality.

In *Three Sisters*, for example, Vershinin drugs himself and others with a lot of very clever words and entertains a lunch party with some fascinating philosophy (well, sort-of fascinating, sort-of philosophy). But probably he is hiding from himself the fact that he's left his small children at home with a suicidal mother. He's dosing himself with words. He's talking nineteen to the dozen because he doesn't want to acknowledge his irresponsibility. The words offer a relief from symptoms. The best way to bamboozle the listener is to use too many syllables to get across too little information. The information–syllable ratio is a powerful tool when you want to bury the truth. Under a barrage of syllables, your attention will start to wander. Each of the words are understandable, but with enough syllables, the listener will lose interest, and getting people to lose interest is a powerful political device. Here, the words aren't about communicating. They are about hiding something.

Othello murders Desdemona under a cascade of words: '*It is the cause, it is the cause, my soul! Let me not name it to you, you chaste stars…*' These are often considered beautiful words. He paints himself as a cosmic champion of virtue. But, as always, let's not leave our common sense at the door. As he intones these words like a liturgy, let's remember that he's planning to strangle a young woman whom he's brought hundreds of miles away from her friends and family. He's committing a shabby, secret murder. So he tries to drug us, and indeed himself, not with chemicals but with words, with hokum, with bullshit. And he must keep on upping the intensity of his verbal hokum as the effect wears off. A classic sign of addiction is when we must increase the dose.

When characters start to talk 'high', we ought to be suspicious, and red warning lights should start flashing in our imaginations: 'Why is he making this so complicated?' Desdemona's line '*Kill me tomorrow, let me live tonight!*' is so heartbreaking, not just because of the simplicity of these ten syllables, but because those tiny words make a pinprick in the middle of his onslaught of text. She shames him linguistically. You don't need all those fancy words to be a human being.

We've seen it already in the way that the Macbeths talk. They come out with all sorts of grandiose language, using euphemisms like '*our great quell*' to mean 'murdering the king'. But in fact they are using words to mask the smell of their self-disgust; as a whiff of air-freshener in a lavatory.

◦— **Pay attention to the distance between what a character is saying and what they are doing.**

A void gapes open between what Vershinin, Macbeth and Othello say and what they do. They often use the words to sanitise, anaesthetise or to distract. They are, essentially, talking bullshit. Which is not to say that bullshit isn't useful to us when we are piecing these characters together. Of course, in rehearsal, we need all these words. When we're working with Shakespeare's plays, they are the only thing we have to work with. They are our forensic evidence about what is happening. What the character says is what they want the world to hear, and what they want to believe about themselves. That doesn't mean that we should believe them. We need to keep a cold eye on their choice of words. We should never be conned by the grandiosity of a character's language. Very often, a character uses words to keep reality at a safe distance.

Often, too, the cleverer and prettier the words, the greater the hokum. Part of Shakespeare's brilliance is his capacity to write bullshit. He must have heard so much. He knows that the more scared and vulnerable we are, the more inflated our words can get as we try to claw back some illusion of control. These characters speak poetically. But that doesn't mean they are more sophisticated than we are. Poetry can feel intimidating. We are taught to believe that prose is normal communication, and when we work with poetic text, by the likes of Shakespeare, or Calderón, or Sophocles, we must somehow elevate ourselves and reach a 'level'. But this is misleading.

Poetry is a very basic part of human interaction. Poetry is where we began. It is dangerous to teach children that prose is somehow 'normal', and that verse is a later fancy add-on, some sort of sophisticated extrapolation of prose. It's the exact reverse. Humans first start with poetry and only then learn prose. When we are born, we communicate with our mothers extremely well before we can make any words at all. It's probably the clearest communication we will ever have with anyone. When language comes between us, that relationship will get a lot more complicated. After vast effort, a whole set of experiences suddenly gets caught in two syllables: 'Mama.' The parents applaud and consider it a triumph that the baby can define its imagination in a single word. Before this first word, the child speaks in noises, wriggling its body, putting syllables together, playing with the sound of things. The first, preverbal utterances that a human being makes are a form of poetry.

As we grow older, we may speak in prose, but we continue to think in poetry. It is a struggle to tie our feelings up into tidy prose bundles. The experience inside our minds is much more to do with epic verse and imagery. Our most intimate thoughts are nothing to do with prose at all. When you open your mouth to say anything important or personal, you need to squeeze that vast epic poetic experience into mundane prose. When we speak to each other about anything important, we are always using a form of Google Translate.

Poetry is something we do naturally. We slip into it all the time, whenever prose fails us. It is very hard to have any ordinary human conversation without some poetry. If someone is annoying you, you might say 'Go away!' If that doesn't work, you might resort to any one of any number of more colourful expressions that I will spare you here. When ordinary language fails, we resort to sound, image and metaphor. This is poetry. Poetry steps in when prose has failed.

It's a disaster to think of Shakespeare's plays as great stories unfortunately wrapped up in archaic poetry, covered in the dust of the past. 'Nice plot, shame about all those words. If only we could strip off the poetry from this rattling good tale, then we'd be just fine and dandy, and you'd expose the great thriller plots that are the real heart of the plays.' But at the end of the day, *Macbeth* is far more than a thriller. *Macbeth* is about many things that defy explanation. If you can explain *Macbeth*, you've killed the play, because the things we can't explain are the most important things to share.

We use poetry for all sorts of human reasons. We need poetry when we need to talk about more than bare facts. We use poetry when prose fails to control the world in the way we need. Above all, we need poetry when we feel lonely and frightened. We are all poets. And so, Shakespeare filled his plays with poets, because he understood this key:

⌐ Poetry is more human than prose.

Let's go back to rehearsal and look at the very end of the play. In this scene, the castle is under siege and Macbeth has just delivered a machismo rallying speech to his soldiers. He tells them he is numb to fear, and ready to face anything. At the end of it, a messenger enters to tell him that Lady Macbeth, tormented by her nightmares, is dead. Macbeth is left in the rubble of that information, his army staring back at him. And he comes out with:

> *'She should have died hereafter;*
> *There would have been a time for such a word.*
> *Tomorrow, and tomorrow, and tomorrow,*
> *Creeps in this petty pace from day to day*
> *To the last syllable of recorded time,*
> *And all our yesterdays have lighted fools*
> *The way to dusty death. Out, out, brief candle!*
> *Life's but a walking shadow, a poor player*
> *That struts and frets his hour upon the stage*
> *And then is heard no more. It is a tale*
> *Told by an idiot, full of sound and fury,*
> *Signifying nothing.'*

Right away, the words don't work. Shakespeare sticks his finger right on the nerve. Macbeth doesn't say, 'There would have been a time for such a *thing.*' He says, '*There would have been a time for such a* word.' The words 'My wife is dead' make no sense to him in that moment. They are absurdly inadequate. He has crossed a threshold and discovered he cannot comprehend the new universe he finds on the other side. His first two lines defy meaning, as Macbeth struggles to put words to this moment. The idea that there could ever be '*a time for such a word*' is logically nonsensical. In its resonant mystery, in its breakdown of meaning, we understand Macbeth's experience far more vividly than the banal meaning of the words can capture. It would be a mistake for Alex to believe this speech is a description of how Macbeth feels. We should not imagine that what is going on here is that Macbeth is opening up to the audience and reaching to the depths of his poetic being to tell us about despair. Macbeth has become accidentally poetic while he is trying to do something else.

So what *is* he trying to do in this speech? Well, perhaps he's using words to run away from his dread. He's trying to make his shabby little end seem epic. It's a speech peppered with braggadocio. Macbeth, as so often in this play, is trying to say: 'The thing about me is that I've got it all sussed out. I know there's no point to living, and I don't care.' He wants to sound clever, fashionably empty of hope. He shits on all life by saying that it is nothing more than '*a tale told by an idiot*'. His despair is a desperate act of self-control. It lets him run away from responsibility. If life is meaningless, and all actions are worthless, then he doesn't have to admit that all of this is really his fault. There's no way that Macbeth's going to do that. He's using words as an anti-panic drug. His position of clever nihilism is a way of putting a straitjacket on the panic and grief boiling away underneath. He can't afford to let us, or the army, or himself, see what he's feeling. He can't afford to start feeling it himself. He would disintegrate.

He's also running away from time. It's as if, for the first time in the whole play, he's trying to stop and think and process. But it's too late to do that now. He might have done so in Act One, but time has been hurtling past Macbeth. It's all gone much, much too fast. And now, suddenly, sickeningly, his wife is dead, and it's as if time itself has stopped. Macbeth can't afford to stop, though, because the enemy is at the door. This is how time works for all of us. Our experience of it is that it goes much too fast, or much too slowly, but never quite at the perfect pace that makes us feel in control. Like the space, time is never fully on our side. This becomes horribly clear as the stakes mount. So Macbeth speaks to us, and to his army, as if he is in control of time. He says he can see forward until '*the last syllable of recorded time*' and pass an all-knowing eye over '*all our yesterdays*'. This, of course, is supreme bullshit.

With these words, Macbeth wants us to know that he is a brilliant pessimist and a master of time who doesn't care two figs about life. But we would be foolish to believe him. What's happening is something completely different. What's happening is that Macbeth is falling apart. Something magical happens as we watch him. This speech is an exquisite piece of poetry, but the extraordinary thing is that Macbeth isn't trying to be poetic. That's the last thing he has time for. And yet he is; astoundingly so. Macbeth has betrayed himself in trying to say something tinny and cynical and hyper-controlled, but the words accidentally blow up into poetry. He is a man who roars at us that he has no feelings, but you see a tear glint at the corner of his eye and hear poetry streaming out of his mouth. His unconscious is, like everybody else's, quite out of his control. It blows up his words. As so often with Macbeth, he speaks better than he knows.

If Alex believes his main task is to mean the words, the speech will be dead to watch. The humanity of this speech only comes to life when we feel the words fail. It comes to life in the vibrating tension between the words Macbeth says and what he is trying to do. It comes to life when factual prose erupts into mysterious poetry.

Words are only clues. Alex will do himself a huge favour if he holds off as long as possible from understanding the meaning of the words he must learn, and instead allows himself to be haunted by them. Haunting is central to our experience of life, of ourselves. It takes over when understanding fails us. It is our reality, which we sometimes paper over with clever understanding. Like stories that become myths, we will only know that something is useful to us if it continues to haunt us, if it takes hold of our imaginations, bothers us, and refuses to be solved or silenced. If we struggle to tame something into understanding, we will probably kill it.

The greatest of modern physicists, who have begun to unravel mysteries at the very heart of the universe, accept that they're never going to understand everything. And perhaps there may be some things that no human will ever understand.

THE POLITICAL ACTOR

16

The moment an actor acts, they send a message to the audience that says: 'Before, I was acting me – but now look! I am acting someone else. Now I see the world this person sees.' The actor creates a world that not only tolerates difference, but also rejoices in the variety of human nature. A world in which we all have the capacity to be many different things. A world that accepts loss, embraces change, recognises ambivalence and endures uncertainty. The sheer act of acting, even without any overtly political message, already constitutes a political act.

The greatest moment in theatre for me is always the same. It is when the actor turns, and sees a new space, and encounters the predicament. At that moment we are equal to the actor. We see through the actor. I remember, when I was very small, in the west of Ireland, a group of aunts holding a blame-shame session over fruit cake. They were dissecting the culprit of some local scandal or other. I vividly recall a moment when one of my many aunts or cousins could suddenly bear it no longer and exploded, saying, 'I don't care what he's done, he's still a human being!' I remember she pronounced 'human' as *yooman*. The angle of her head, the flash in her eyes, the crack in her voice were unforgettable – because I saw what she saw, and saw it from her position. Later on, I came to realise that what I noticed then was that theatre isn't just about watching a character. It's about seeing someone see something else. I saw that she saw the world from a unique position. I saw that she had a point of view that might be different from other people's, from mine, and, for a second, I was able to see the space through another pair of eyes. It was different from seeing something in a different way. It was as if I were standing in another pair of shoes.

We've been doing this as long as art has existed. Think of a prehistoric cave painting of a hunter and a mammoth. We look at the mammoth seeing the puny hunter, and we also see the little stick-figure hunter with the spear facing down this huge animal. We see the hunter seeing the mammoth. We see the mammoth through the hunter's eyes. And we see the mammoth seeing him. We imagine what life looks like from where each of them is standing. Theatre, as with all art, comes from our ability not just to connect to something outside us, but to stand concretely in another's position: most concretely, in someone else's shoes.

It transcends what is 'inside' the writer, or the director, or the actor. It is about the electricity in the space between. This is what makes theatre compulsive. We watch the character – be they Macbeth, my Aunt Mary or the cave-dweller – encountering a massive predicament in the space. We see it through them. As a result, we are part of the creation. We have conceived something between us and have become complicit in this act of imagination.

As the actor turns and sees the predicament, we are caught in a thrillingly unstable Limbo. It's a moment when, even if we know the same old text by heart, it seems as if anything could happen. With great gulps of oxygen, together with the actor, we stare freedom in the face. We know what it feels like to be a sandcastle facing the tide. For a moment, we feel less lonely.

And then the actor reacts.

17

THE
KEYS

Here are the keys used in this book. Use them only if they prove useful. Chuck them out if they're not. Better still, design your own. It goes without saying that these keys are not a mechanical solution to every problem in rehearsal. They are not actually keys, but they are worth considering. Then put them back in your pocket and play.

- A character is always trying to fix the space.

- The space is never neutral.

- The space is always changing, so the character is never in control.

- Pay attention to your common-sense alarm.

- Get horizontal with the character.

- There is no acting, only reacting to the space.

- The space dictates how the character will behave.

- Acting isn't about transforming yourself. It's about swapping spaces with your character.

- Every soliloquy is a conversation with the audience.

- All characters are unreliable narrators.

- All characters are putting on a performance of themselves.

- The space isn't just outside us. It's also inside our heads.

- Feelings come from outside us.

- We work against the space and our emotions.

- All characters have a problem with themselves.

- Listen carefully for anything that is loud by its absence.

- Characters quarantine space.

- Look for what is over there that is making here dangerous.

- The scene next door is more important than this one.

- Every change is a threshold.

- Crossing a threshold means meeting a surprise.

- You cannot cross a threshold and remain the same.

- The space is always in flux.

- Attend to the flow.

- You can't let anything new into your brain until you make space for it.

- Only the space can bring the character into life.

- Don't think about who your character is. Think about what your character sees.

- Ask questions starting with 'what/where/who', not 'how/why'.

- Look for predicament.

- The character often feels as if they have found themselves in the wrong space.

- Don't search for what the character wants. Look for what they dread.

- Words fail.

- Pay attention to the distance between what a character is saying and what they are doing.

- Poetry is more human than prose.

ACKNOWLEDGEMENTS

This book has been in gestation for twenty years and many people have given us encouragement. Some have read early drafts and, of course, many of the theatre-makers I know or have worked with have provided invaluable insights. In alphabetical order, Vinícius Albricker, Grace Andrews, Valérie Bezançon, Francesco Bianchi, Paul Brennan, Josete Corral, Paddy Cunneen, Dina Dodina, Eamon Farren, Sophie Fiennes, Ignacio García May, Jane Gibson, Judith Greenwood, Scott Handy, Owen Horsley, Orlando James, Patric Knutsson, Anya Kolesnikova, Gabor Koltai, Frances Lawrence, Claudiu Mihail, Carl Miller, Marcus Roche, Laurentiu Tudor, Vlad Udrescu, Andrew Upton, Arantxa Vela and Lydia Wilson.

I am deeply grateful for the support and encouragement of Fiona Williams, Matt Applewhite and Nick Hern.

Declan Donnellan
London, 2024

LUCIE DAWKINS

Lucie Dawkins is a director and freelance curator, who trained at the David Geffen School of Drama at Yale. She is the co-founder of SCRUM Theatre and she produces and hosts the podcast *Not True, But Useful...* with Declan Donnellan and Nick Ormerod for Cheek by Jowl. Lucie lectures in theatre at the Barbican and Guildhall School of Music and Drama, and facilitates Shakespeare workshops for children both at the Guildhall and through the Coram Shakespeare Schools Foundation. She is a translator of Greek tragedies, most often for Cheek by Jowl. Beyond the theatre, she produces digital and audio projects for museums, most recently for the Ashmolean, who also published her book, *Museum Secrets*.

INDEX

absence 64, 73–6, 93–5, 106, 135, 179, 203–4, 223
advertisements 87, 145, 187
ambiguity and ambivalence 31, 104, 168, 203, 219
Andrei (*Three Sisters*) 94
Apollo 28
As You Like It 87
authenticity 143–6

babies 13, 60–2, 72, 75, 83–4, 107–8, 123, 138, 150, 166, 187, 190, 204, 210–11
Banquo (*Macbeth*) 78, 138, 173–4, 180, 192, 196–8
Beatrice (*Much Ado About Nothing*) 66, 170–2, 177, 192
Beckett, Samuel 170, 173
Bede, the Venerable 147–8
Benedick (*Much Ado About Nothing*) 66, 170–2, 192
Boétie, Étienne de la 205–6
bullshit 80–1, 128, 197, 209–10, 214

Cabaret 66
Calderón de la Barca, Pedro 210
Caravaggio 104–5
character 9–10, 14–17, 28–33, 39–42, 46–8, 57–9, 65–7, 73–6, 87, 102–3, 106–7, 124, 129–31, 138–60, 163–70, 178–81, 185–92, 199, 205, 209–10, 219–20, 223–4
Chekhov, Anton 74, 93–5, 191–2, 208–9
children and childhood 7–8, 14–17, 21, 45–6, 59, 65, 71, 75, 99, 107, 119, 126–7, 136, 166–7, 188, 198, 203–5, 210–11; *see also* babies
Chorus Line, A 56–7

circumstances 163–6, 170, 173
Claudius (*Hamlet*) 57, 179, 199
comedy 66, 170–1, 190; *see also* tragedy
common-sense alarm 21–3, 43, 45, 75–9, 82, 138, 178, 190–1, 208–9, 223
Constance (*King John*) 203–4
control 15–23, 30, 43, 48, 55, 60–3, 78, 81–4, 101–3, 107–9, 117, 122–6, 129, 137–40, 143–4, 150, 155, 160, 164, 168, 173, 179, 186–9, 196–9, 203–6, 210–15, 223
Cornwall (*King Lear*) 169

Davis, Bette 54
Desdemona (*Othello*) 28, 165, 172–3, 199, 208–9
Dionysus 28
'dis-experiencing' 208
dread 45, 62, 130, 169, 171, 183–99, 213, 224
dreams and nightmares 21, 84, 128, 150–2, 157–9, 165, 169, 172, 212

Edgar (*King Lear*) 206
egg-splatter 102
Eliot, T. S. 207
Emilia (*Othello*) 172–3
emotions 9, 13, 53–62, 65, 67, 71–2, 75, 78–9, 82–4, 127–30, 145, 149, 156, 160, 165, 189, 194–7, 204, 211, 213–15, 223
empathy 58, 74, 166–9, 181, 204, *see also* sympathy
encounters and encountering 29, 104–6, 160, 166, 206, 219–20

Fabergé eggs 137, 146
failure 9, 16–20, 42, 48, 56, 75–6, 80, 84, 125, 130, 190, 199, 204–7, 211–12, 215, 224
false friends 25–33, 53
false words 201–15
feelings, *see* emotions
film 22, 46, 54, 73, 92, 99–100, 102, 135, 166
fish 4, 9
flow 13, 131–40, 143, 224
flux 15, 124–6, 143, 224; *see also* flow
futility 54, 204–5; *see also* failure

Gertrude (*Hamlet*) 57, 73–4, 179
'getting horizontal' 28–9, 150, 165, 223
ghosts and haunting 21, 48, 60–2, 84, 108, 118, 121, 123–5, 127, 165, 188, 203–4, 215
Gloucester (*King Lear*) 169–70
green glasses 35–49, 164, 167
Gwendolen (*The Importance of Being Earnest*) 190–1

Hamlet 57, 73–4, 148–9, 165, 179, 199, 205
Hamlet (*Hamlet*) 57, 73–4, 148–9, 165, 179, 199, 205
Happy Days 173
'here' 14, 23, 60, 71, 75, 83, 87–92, 99, 118–122, 224; *see also* 'there'
horizontality, *see* 'getting horizontal'
horror films 22, 46
'how' and 'why' questions 149–52, 154–7, 160, 185, 224; *see also* 'who/what/where' questions

'I' and 'me' 65–7, 82, 129, 143–4, 148, 219
Iago (*Othello*) 173
ideas 61–7, 83–4, 92–3, 122, 129, 137, 140, 143–6, 150, 164, 168–9, 203

Importance of Being Earnest, The 190–1
improvisation 7, 101, 102, 135, 138
inclusion and exclusion 45, 69–84, 94–5, 109, 129–30; *see also* quarantine
'inner life' 53–4
'invisible work' 138–40, 172
Irina (*Three Sisters*) 74, 191

Jaws 166
jeopardy 104–5, 164, 180; *see also* predicament
Juliet (*Romeo and Juliet*) 93, 169, 189

Kane, Sarah 170
Kant, Immanuel 41
keys 13, 32, 43, 105, 111–31, 150, 178, 192, 212, 221–4
Kierkegaard, Søren 140
King John 203–4
King Kong 56
King Lear 169–70, 206

Lady Bracknell (*The Importance of Being Earnest*) 192
Lady Macbeth, see *Macbeth*
Lear (*King Lear*) 206
logic and illogic 19–20, 27–8, 82–3, 128, 144, 157, 185, 195, 203–4, 213
'Love Song of J. Alfred Prufrock, The' 207

Macbeth 4, 56, 75, 87, 99, 138, 148–9, 172, 185–6, 189–90, 198–9, 209, 211–12, 220; 'Ay, in the catalogue ye go for men' 173–81; 'Great Glamis! Worthy Cawdor!' 62–7; 'If it were done when 'tis done' 76–84; 'If we should fail?' 88–92, 102–10; 'Is this a dagger?' 17–23, 27–8, 31–2, 157; 'My single state of man'

144–5; 'O, full of scorpions is my mind' 192–9; 'Out, damned spot!' 150–60, 164–5; 'This is a sorry sight' 113–31, 150–1; 'Tomorrow, and tomorrow, and tomorrow' 212–15; 'Unsex me here' 37–49, 53–4, 58–61, 72, 151; 'Who can be wise?' 144–5
Macbeth, see *Macbeth*
mammoths 219–20
meaning 48, 80, 203–9, 213–15
memory and memories 59–61, 65, 67, 72, 75, 82, 108, 118–19, 122, 127–8, 139, 158, 165, 172
Miss Prism (*The Importance of Being Earnest*) 190–1
monologue, *see* soliloquy
Montaigne, Michel de 205–6
Moscow Art Theatre 74
Much Ado About Nothing 66, 170–2, 177, 192
murderers (*Macbeth*) 173–81

Natasha (*Three Sisters*) 94
Newton, Isaac 32
'next door' 78, 88, 91–5, 99, 106, 123, 224
Nietzsche, Friedrich 189
nightmares, *see* dreams and nightmares
nuclear buttons 75, 108
Nurse (*Romeo and Juliet*) 93

Olivia (*Twelfth Night*) 55
Orsino (*Twelfth Night*) 55
Othello 28, 165, 172–3, 199, 208–9
Othello (*Othello*) 28, 165, 172–3, 199, 208–9
other people's shoes 28, 41, 149, 167–8, 177, 191, 219–20; *see also* empathy

photography 73
Pinter, Harold 170

'plugging in' 9–10, 53–4, 160
Poe, Edgar Allan 8–9
poetry 21, 30, 73, 81, 84, 119, 125, 168, 210–15, 224
politics and politicians 77, 81, 208, 217–20
predicament 161–81, 187, 191, 199, 219–20, 224
Proust, Marcel 59
psychiatry and psychoanalysis 27–9, 91, 117, 121

quarantine 70–84, 108, 129–30, 223

realism and the 'realistic' 29–30, 104
Regan (*King Lear*) 169
Romeo (*Romeo and Juliet*) 93, 169, 189
Romeo and Juliet 4, 93, 169, 189, 205
Roosevelt, Franklin D. 188
Rosalind (*As You Like It*) 87

samovars 33
sandcastles 11–23, 71, 88, 94–5, 99, 126, 137, 220
Shakespeare William 21, 22, 28, 43, 56–8, 64, 66, 78, 80–1, 104, 121, 146–9, 152, 169–170, 172, 177–9, 205–6, 210–13; *and see under individual plays and characters*
shoes, *see* other people's shoes
soliloquy 17, 27, 38–9, 43–5, 48, 57–9, 66–7, 76–8, 84, 124, 205, 223
Sophocles 210
Stanislavsky, Konstantin 74, 163
superiority 28–9, 31, 94–5, 149, 160
surprise and surprises 55, 67, 100–7, 110, 185, 224
sympathy 166–8; *see also* empathy

'there' 87–8, 99, 118–23, 149, 191, 224; *see also* 'here'
Three Sisters 74, 93–5, 191–2, 208–9
thresholds 96–110, 138, 157–60, 213, 224
time 15–16, 23, 82, 91, 94–5, 124–5, 140, 146, 165, 187, 212–14
Tom and Jerry 147
tragedy 28, 78, 170–1, 199; *see also* comedy
'truth' 4, 29–31, 41, 67, 143, 145–6, 204, 207–8
Tusenbach (*Three Sisters*) 74
Twelfth Night 55, 87, 179

understanding 8, 16, 27, 31, 41, 56, 92–3, 128, 167–9, 186, 203, 215

Vershinin (*Three Sisters*) 94, 208–9
'vesting' 188–9, 198–9
Viola (*Twelfth Night*) 87, 179
violence 30, 73–4, 81, 145, 172, 186

war 62, 64, 101, 167
'who/what/where' questions 88, 149–60, 185, 195–6, 224; *see also* 'how' and 'why' questions
Wilde, Oscar 190–1
Winnie (*Happy Days*) 173
witches (*Macbeth*) 21, 37, 56, 108, 123, 144
words 9, 13, 21–2, 29–31, 44, 48, 59, 64, 73, 75, 79–81, 100–1, 120, 129, 138, 148, 158, 163–4, 180, 196, 200–15, 224; *see also* false words

www.nickhernbooks.co.uk

facebook.com/nickhernbooks
twitter.com/nickhernbooks